IF GOD IS MY FATHER, HOW CAN HE LOVE ME?

IF GOD IS MY FATHER, HOW CAN HE LOVE ME?

Celia Haddon

Hodder & Stoughton

Copyright © Celia Haddon 1998

First published in Great Britain 1998

The right of Celia Haddon to be identified as the author of the
Work has been asserted by her in accordance with the Copyright,
Designs and Patents Act 1988

10 9 8 7 6 5 4 3 2 1

British Library Cataloguing in Publication Data
A record for this book is available from the British Library

ISBN 0 340 71394 1

Design and computer page make up
Penny & Tony Mills

Printed and bound in Great Britain
Clays Ltd, St Ives PLC

Hodder and Stoughton
A Division of Hodder Headline PLC
338 Euston Road
London NW1 3BH

To Pamela,
with thanks for her wise words

CONTENTS

	Introduction	9
1	The Unhealed Wounded	13
2	Learning to Love	31
3	Mild, Obedient, Good as He	48
4	The Everlasting Fires	65
5	A Damnable Doctrine	75
6	The Devices and Desires of My Own Heart	92
7	Don't Care, Can't Care	109
8	Give it a Whirl	124
9	A Kind of Civil Confession	141
10	Being Good, Being Nice and Being Perfect	157
11	Damned Below Judas	173
12	A Deep and Dazzling Darkness	191

INTRODUCTION

My father was dying. His breath was so slight that I could no longer hear it, and I would get up from beside the bed and look to see if he had stopped breathing altogether. If a feather had been held to his thin sunken lips, it would scarcely have trembled. But just as it seemed that the breath would die away completely, his chest would heave. The lungs would struggle to draw three or four harsh long intakes of life-giving air. Then slowly these would fade back to only threadlike breathing.

The body was struggling to go on living. The heart was beating despite the stroke that had robbed him of speech and perhaps of hearing. The rib cage would shudder as the lungs fought to keep taking in air. Like bellows, they kept pumping – nearly stopping, then starting up again with a series of gasps. For hours, then for days, then for more than a week this pattern of fading breath, followed by harsh gasping, continued. He did not seem to hear words any more. He lay in the large sitting room of the West Country farmhouse, where he had come home from hospital. From the wall, pictures of horses and dogs stared down at the slowly dying body – the two jockeys riding out their thoroughbreds with a cat on the wall behind them, the gentleman farmer astride his horse in a Leicestershire landscape with a church spire on the horizon, the two pointers frozen in paint chasing a hare across a field.

On the floor the living pointer dog, old Sam, lay in front of the empty fire. In dog age, Sam was as old as his owner and so stiff from arthritis that he found it difficult to struggle to his feet. He would be chasing no more hares. The summer of 1990 was hot. Warm sunlight slanted in through the French windows near the bed. Grace, the attendant nurse, wiped the dying man's forehead and wet his dried lips. He could no longer swallow and his tongue would occasionally pass round his lips in search of the water which unconsciously he still craved.

He was dying from the aftermath of the stroke. He was dying from the mortification of his leg that was turning black and smelling. Only the district nurse's careful bandaging kept off the flies. He was dying from starvation. He was dying from thirst. But oh, how he fought it. He had been a strong man. Too strong now for an easy death.

I think that he had known that his death was approaching very close. For three months I had visited him two or three times a week in the hospital, but we did not speak of his forthcoming death.

Once, I thought he might talk about it. 'The good thing about having a stroke is that it doesn't hurt at all,' he said. Then he added: 'I don't think my chances of getting out of here are very good. What do you think?' Carefully, I said: 'People recover from strokes. It is hard work for them, but they can relearn how to move again. I think if you work hard at it, you can get out of here.' There was a pause. He changed the subject. So we did not talk about death. Did he want to? I do not know. There was so much we could not talk about.

Once, a local vicar from the church near the geriatric hospital came to visit him. He sat on the end of the hospital bed. 'I didn't say anything. I wouldn't talk to him,' said my father. 'He just sat there for five minutes and left'. Years before, he had joked: 'I don't believe any of it. But when I am dying I shall get myself converted, just to be on the safe side.' But now he knew that death was approaching and he didn't do so. He stayed true to himself, to his unbending disbelief. Perhaps he would not even say hello to the vicar in case he was tempted to waver. He had held on to his integrity in the face of death.

He had got out of there eventually. He had come home to die. It was as if the effort of arguing his way out of hospital had used up all his strength, and as soon as he arrived he began to weaken fast. Now his face lay back on the pillow. The nose was sharpening, the eyes sinking back into their hollows, the lips thin and wasted. The skull beneath the skin showed more clearly every hour.

I put my hand into his hand which was lying outside the bedclothes. The motionless fingers did not close on mine. Even a dying man might close his fingers, if a friendly hand slips into his. It is a natural gesture. When my father's hand did not close on mine, I thought that he must be completely unable to know me, unconscious, unhearing, unfeeling. But I could not be sure. Would my father have held my hand, anyway, even if he had been conscious? Would he have thought the gesture too intimate? To hold somebody's hand is a childhood gesture of trust. Did my father trust? Could he? Ever?

For eight days he lay dying. The only word he spoke was to the gentle nurse, Grace, who was looking after him.

'Sweetheart', he breathed. But for his family there were no words. And we, not knowing the etiquette of death and unable to think of what it might be, or indeed, to think at all, had few words for him. We did not speak to him. We watched him. That was all.

I wish it had been different.

But then I wish everything that was between my father and me had been different. I loved him. I still love him. By the time of his death, he loved me in his own way.

The relationship between my father and me has spread through my whole life, giving it a distinctive pattern which spreads right through my work, my existing family and my God. If God is my father, I can love him but I cannot speak truthfully to him. I can love him, but I cannot trust him. I can love him, but I will always fear him too. And if God is my father, then how can he love me?

CHAPTER ONE

THE UNHEALED
WOUNDED

The story of my spiritual life begins with my father, Darby Haddon. I have an oil painting of him on the wall of my staircase landing. He is mounted on Thunder, his favourite bay hunter, and he is looking out over the Cotswold hills of his farm. He is smartly dressed in black top hat, white stock, red hunting coat, white kid breeches, and black leather boots. The cost of horse and equipment must have been the equivalent of a small car. His expression is far sighted, stern but distant, and he is sitting up straight in the saddle, not at all as he did in real life. In real life he slumped in the saddle with all the relaxation of a man at peace with himself. Truly, I think he was only at peace with himself when he was galloping recklessly across the grassland, jumping stone walls, hedges, and fences, or facing a particularly big obstacle, turning to his friends and laughing, 'I'll go first and knock the top off for you.' He was a fearless rider and a dangerous father.

At the time of my birth in 1944 he was not looking forward to my arrival in this world. My mother had gone back to her parents' home in Cambridge to give birth to me because their marriage was in crisis. It was not certain whether she would ever return to live with him. In today's society they would have separated at this point, if they had not done so earlier. But in 1944 divorce was a social disgrace and both of them were very conscious of that. They stayed together for sixteen more pain-filled years, both of them making an already bad relationship worse.

If I could have sensed my father's attitude from my cradle, and perhaps babies can, I would have detected his lack of enthusiasm for me from the very beginning. What has this to do with my spiritual life? Well, the Christian tradition is to pray to a God, who is our father. So as children, we imagine a God who is like the only father we know, our real earthly father or father figure. And for some of us, the metaphor designed to attract and reassure us becomes an image which distresses us, makes us anxious, or even repels us.

My father's brooding anger hung over my whole childhood. We children were as much in awe of him as if he was God (and we were perhaps even more frightened). In his daily life he was, if not almighty, then very nearly so. A tall man usually dressed for farming days in a check shirt and corduroy trousers, with a spotted red handkerchief sometimes holding them up instead of a belt, he moved with perfect physical co-ordination. His body language was that of a man who was complete master of his environment. When he sat down in the armchair, he sprawled there reading the paper with his dogs at his feet gazing up at him spellbound. They adored him as their pack leader, recognising and enjoying his overwhelming authority. And we, his family, recognised and feared that same authority.

A prosperous farmer, he employed nine farm workers, a mechanic, a foreman and two grooms. In the house was a day cook, two cleaning women and an old age pensioner who shined the family shoes. In the village where we lived when I was growing up, there were only three farms and about three houses bigger than ours, which was called the Manor Farm. The three farmers, the families in the Grange, the Manor House, and the big house on the green, were the core gentry of the village. One or two retired people, the occasional commuter, unmarried middle class women and widows, and the vicar, were next in the social order. Then there were the shopkeepers, the skilled craftsmen and what in those days middle class people without embarrassment called 'the working classes'. All the farm workers had considerable skills, but they were nonetheless classified merely as workers, not craftsmen.

My father was completely autonomous in his own world. He hired and fired at will, without the legal restrictions of today. Strangely, he was better as an employer than as a family man, kinder to those outside the house than to those inside, usually fair even generous except for his occasional rages. These were terrifying. I have seen the men on the farm grow pale under the lash of his cruel tirade.

As well as running a large arable farm, he also became the chairman and chief shareholder of the family firm, Dormans, which made diesel engines. As soon as his elderly mother had made over the voting shares to him, he was all-powerful there too. His first act was to fire the managing director and one of the directors who had somehow not given him the respect he thought he deserved. His next was to buy several Savile Row suits and acquire a Rolls Royce car from the firm. Thus kitted out, he would motor up the poor 1950s roads to Staffordshire where, as managing director, he would also fire any other senior figures who incurred his wrath. My mother would have anxious calls, after he had set out, from his employees (to call them colleagues would be a misnomer) asking what kind of mood he was in. They were frightened of him too.

Only in one area of his life was that power limited. The real business of his life was foxhunting. At times when he was running the family business he could manage only four or five days' hunting a week, because unfortunately for him no hunt went out on a Sunday. Later, when he sold the family business, he hunted six days a week and would undoubtedly have hunted for seven days if only that had been possible. His physical energy was amazing.

The ancient ritual of foxhunting required the expensive outfit which is so impressive in his portrait. On the hunting field, however, he had to defer to two higher authorities, the Master of Foxhounds and the Field Master, who was in charge of the followers on horseback. My father was a hard rider, with a remarkable lack of fear. When he dislocated his shoulder out hunting, he simply continued with his arm in a sling. He enjoyed risk and usually refused medical treatment, often using horse liniment instead of human medicine. At the age of seventy, he fell off his horse and was knocked unconscious. When he came to, in a car being driven to hospital, he refused to go to the casualty department. Instead, he persuaded them just to take him home and put him to bed, not letting them know that my stepmother was away and he therefore was on his own. Without any medical attention at all, he simply got up the following morning and carried on with life. In normal circumstances the hunting field brought out the best in him, even though this was the only area of his life where he had to obey others.

The Unhealed Wounded

I do not know whether power always creates fear. Is it natural to fear those who control our destinies? Is it inevitable to fear those who seem to control all around them? It is, to me. I only know that my chief feeling towards my father was that of fear. My mother feared him too. To my childish eyes, everybody feared him as much as I did and everybody was wary around him. I did not know, as I know now, that the unhealed wounded are dangerous to be near.

In summer, when he left the house to go and look round the farm, the atmosphere inside would perceptibly lighten. In winter, when he left to go foxhunting, a sense of even greater relief spread round the house. Off in the horsebox with the girl groom, two horses in the back so that he could change from one to another at half time, he would be away till teatime. There would be no chance of meeting him in the stableyard, or running across him in the garden. Lunch would be a peaceful meal without arguments. The day would stretch ahead without fear. Until late afternoon, that is. Then, as the lights were switched on and the heavy kettle put on the Aga for tea, my anxiety would rise.

Soon after he would walk into the kitchen with its polished red flagstones. He would smell of horses, and his white breeches would be stained and the shine on his leather hunting boots dulled with equine sweat. Perhaps he would drink a cup of tea before hurling violent abuse at my mother. More probably he would abuse her before finishing the first cup. 'You're a useless tool. Nothing in your head except feathers. I gave you a little job to do and you've made a mess of it.'

I would either slink out of the kitchen, or try to divert him from the row I saw coming, by asking if he had had a good day. It was impossible to know in advance what might be his reaction to my well-meant conversational efforts. It might stave off his anger with my mother or it might bring the anger on me instead. His anger was not only frightening but it was also completely unpredictable. To live with him required a state of constant alertness, a continuous checking of small cues like the tone of his voice or the change in his expression. That he would be angry with my mother was inevitable. Not a single meal went by without at least a few cutting remarks and, more often, a full-scale row. But by careful understanding of the nuances of his body language and tone of voice, it was sometimes possible to delay his anger, at least for a little while.

He was also unpredictable in his likings and dislikings. A favoured person could, in his eyes, suddenly become an object of hatred if they disagreed with him. And when this happened he did not hesitate. Unable to cope with any kind of emotional confrontation, he violently cut them out of his life. There would be no explanation, no search or research into the cause of the difficulty and, above all, no turning back. Forgiveness might have impelled him to reassess the hurtful incident or the offender's character, or even his part in the disagreement. This he could not face. So there was no forgiveness. I don't think he ever forgot a slight and I know that he never forgave one.

At one point he quarrelled with a former close friend, a Master of Foxhounds. In a violent rage, my father had ordered him never to set foot on his land again. Twenty years passed. While the Master's anger had ceased years ago, my father's ban, not on the foxhounds themselves, but on the Master of the hunt, remained in place throughout and resulted in something of a triumph for him a few months before his last illness. The hounds had chased a fox into my father's farmyard and killed it there. The Master had been left sitting on his horse at the foot of the farm drive, unable to enter. Only the hunt servants followed the hounds in. Trying for a reconciliation the Master sent my father the dead fox's head, stuffed and mounted and labelled 'In Memory of Happy Days'.

'Have you thanked him?' I asked my father. For a moment I wondered if the feud might be forgiven. He had clearly been pleased by the stuffed fox head. 'Of course not,' said my father. Twenty years had not diminished his anger in the least, and so the ban continued until his death. (Naturally, when the farm was sold, hunt meets were reinstated there.) Neither the passage of time nor the conciliation of his opponent could elicit forgiveness. He would not let go. His angry judgment, once made, was made for ever.

This applied to the family, too. One of the directors of the family business was the brother of his sister's husband. My father fired him and he and his sister did not speak for the next thirty years. Their only encounters were when he was visiting his mother. As he drove out of the gloomy Victorian mansion, his estranged sister would be waiting in her car outside. Then she would drive at him, in the hope of crashing into him. My father, who enjoyed jumping impossible obstacles on the horse, used to enjoy this too. To him, it had just the right amount of danger to make it a diverting episode, and thanks to his skill at the wheel, she never managed to make a hit. Perhaps because he always came out on top in these thrilling encounters, he made the only exception to his rule of never forgetting or forgiving in her case. He didn't forget, but he found the memory amusing rather than painful. After thirty years of silence between them, he spoke to her and visited her a couple of times before his death. He was conscious of his magnanimity and made many jokes to me about going soft in his old age.

But he never forgave a close cousin with whom he had quarrelled. Even at his last illness she was missing among the visitors. She wanted to come and see him, but he had cast her out of the family.

A few months before he died, I was visiting him in the crumbling Victorian workhouse, which the Taunton hospital authority had changed into a geriatric hospital. It was a grim place. Though the nursing staff were good, one of the auxiliary helpers worked in the spirit of Victorian benevolence – that is, surreptitiously bullying the patients she was meant to care for. My father was there for weeks, hating it.

In the gloomy little male ward, I told him our cousin wanted to see him. 'I don't want to see her,' he said. 'I shall never forgive her, for what she did.' He blamed her for the break-up of his marriage. This absurd interpretation of his marriage failure presumably in some way lessened his hurt about it. It must have soothed his pride. My cousin had been present at the last horrible row, during which my mother had given her reasons for leaving. She had witnessed his greatest moment of humiliation. This may well have been the reason why he would never forgive her. She had seen his shame. Therefore, in his eyes she could not be forgiven.

He was also unforgiving to animals. He broke several

20

canes by beating his horses around the head with them, when they refused a fence. He wore spurs, a sign either of an old-fashioned rider or one not over-concerned about kindness to his mount. Most of the spurs were just metal prods, but one set had little round spikes so that they would draw blood, not just bruise the skin of the horse's flanks. He wore these for 'difficult' horses.

Did he feel for the animals in his care? Sometimes. I don't think he would have kept battery hens. But he was willing to cause animals suffering, if it increased his profits. In the 1950s he kept a herd of milking cows and he decided that they should lose their horns. In itself this was a sensible decision, for he planned to keep them in a yard during the winter months. But he called in, not the vet, but the cow doctor. In those days there were still cow doctors and horse doctors, unqualified people who treated animals but who no longer had access to veterinary prescription drugs. They were much cheaper than vets.

For two days the large concrete cow yard was full of animals making mournful and unhappy moos. For as each cow was put in a sort of cage, in which they could not move, let alone escape, their horns were cut off without anaesthetic. Blood dripped down their faces. I could not bear to watch this being done, though I heard their cries of pain. Afterwards, I went to see them, fascinated by the horror of it all. The blood had dried and they were recovered enough to eat. Such sights must have been common in the 1930s, when my father started farming. But they were not common in the 1950s and I knew that my father was a rich farmer, not a poor one. He could have afforded a vet with anaesthetics.

His jokes could be cruel ones, too. 'If a son shall ask bread of any of you that is a father, will he give him a stone? or if he ask a fish, will he for a fish give him a serpent?' asked Jesus Christ. Well, my father would never have failed in his duties to feed his children, but he might well have thought giving a snake instead of a fish was a joke. He once invited a four-year-old boy to go and see something very exciting. Sensing something horrible, the child at first refused but was persuaded to follow him by my father's reassurances. The something wonderful turned out to be a mummified dead cat. For years afterwards the boy had nightmares about this cat, nightmares triggered, I believe, as much by adult betrayal as by the horrifying sight itself.

I loved my father and I feared him. As a child, I probably feared him more than I loved him. That fear continued until the age of thirty-three, when I married my husband. It only vanished when I saw him through my husband's eyes – an eccentric but amusing old gentleman farmer, not all-powerful and not always angry. I began to understand that much of his simmering resentment had been the result of a festering marriage and untreated diabetes, and that, in old age, married to a more suitable wife, he was far less disposed to violent rages. He softened in his later years enough to call in a vet to put down his dogs, rather than taking them out and shooting them, himself.

As a father loves his children, so he loved all three of us. Yet this love, that he undoubtedly felt, was expressed only intermittently – in the giving of presents, especially books. Only in these was his love for me made manifest. Now he is dead, I understand why this was and why, in particular, he seemed to hold me of very little account. But as a child, I did not understand. Did I even know that he loved me? I think not. I was the second daughter and a sickly child. As he pointed out to me many times, 'You're the runt of the litter. We didn't think we'd raise you.'

I knew about the litter runts. We kept pigs. The runt, the Tantony pig, the smallest and weakest of the litter, always went for slaughter. The better pigs, kept for a time to fatten them, might be kept for breeding. The runt never was. It is not surprising that I have no children. I had been told I was not fit to breed from. I used to spend hours trying to feed up the runts – a difficult task for an eight-year-old surrounded by milling piglets – in the hope that they might escape slaughter.

I was also a girl. If I had been a boy, I would have borne a name chosen beforehand by him. Because I was a girl, there was no name waiting for me, nor was he much concerned what it might be. My mother chose my name. They had already had one girl, my elder sister. A completely surplus second daughter was not what they wanted. 'Women!' said my father with scorn. 'Give them a place to put down their handbag, and they'll be completely happy. You can get them doing any really boring job.' He did not like women in general and he disliked my mother in particular.

One of my earliest memories of prayer, is the time when my mother was pregnant. My father, a committed atheist, suggested I pray at the side of their big double bed. I was to pray that the next child was a boy – unlike me. This time, after two failures, they were to be blessed with the real thing. 'I believe in primogeniture,' he was to explain later, in 1989, as he left the major part of his fortune to his grandson in the male line. As a child I knew that he despised me. I was of no importance to him, and I knew that furthermore I was a disappointment. For strength and boldness were what he required of his children, as of himself. Designated 'the runt of the litter', I spent most of my first six years being ill. I knew, as I lay in my bed eating the Marmite sandwiches brought upstairs by my mother, that downstairs he was probably grumbling at my weakness. I do not remember if he ever came upstairs to see me in bed. It seems unlikely.

'It's a great life if you never weaken,' he would say and, indeed, in his last illnesses he would not allow any friends to visit him. Then at the last, as throughout his earlier life, he did not want the outside world to see his weakness. Perhaps he thought his ill child would prefer to stay apart in the same way. And truly he was right. I feared him so much that time spent away from him was less worrying than time spent with him.

I disappointed him, too, in physical courage. I was a coward and a wimp and – his chosen term for me – 'the milksop of the family'. I was terrified of horses. My elder sister rode the wild and unsuitable ponies he bought for her with verve and courage. My younger brother was also a courageous rider. I held back and eventually refused to ride at all. This increased his contempt for me. Not only was I not a boy, I was not even a tomboy. 'The gas fire girl', he called me, because of the long hours I spent lying on my stomach reading by the fire. 'You're the cuckoo in the nest,' he declared, a phrase which I then took to mean that I was a family failure on the horse.

Tears brought out the worst in him. During the vicious family arguments round the dining table, I would sometimes

24

burst into tears. 'Here come the waterworks,' he would sneer at the eight-year-old. 'I'll hang two jam jars round your neck and see which fills up first.' I did not know then, as I know now, that he had been so hurt as a child that the only way he could survive was to hurt others. I knew simply that a father was the last person to whom you confided unhappiness or showed sorrow. For if you did, instead of comfort came abuse. It was impossible to trust him for emotional support.

As one of two despised girls, I eventually found a place in the family. I became my brother's keeper, a role that was easy because he was a charming and endearing little boy. During these years I can only remember four occasions when I was alone with my father. Time with him was usually spent with my more important little brother in tow. An early photograph shows me dressed like my little brother. I am wearing the same T-shirt and shorts that he wore, even though five years separated us. It was, I think, a sort of blurring of my less important identity into his. Perhaps even a compliment of kinds. My mother thought of us as a couple, and as most of my time was spent with him, so we became one. She may also have felt that by dressing me like him, the resemblance between us was enhanced. I was, clearly and unmistakably, his sister.

One of the most painful incidents of my childhood occurred when my little brother and I were sitting on the bonnet of the Landrover, being driven over the corn stubble by my father. This was one of the great treats of harvest time. It was very exciting to feel the wind on our faces as we bounced up and down over the uneven ground. Suddenly the Landrover went over a huge hole. My brother fell forwards. I fell sideways. Taking a split-second decision, my father drove on, catching my little brother on the bonnet rather than driving over him. Luckily, I had fallen clear of the vehicle. My father had taken the right decision – neither child was seriously hurt. But while he knew that he had to continue driving in order to catch my brother, he could not have known that I would fall clear. He had chosen to save my brother, at possible risk to me. He explained it all to me, but I felt then that his split-second decision revealed where his heart lay. It made clear the relative importance of us two children. When I look into my own heart, the pain of that summer evening is still with me.

At least I was useful. I was no longer surplus to requirements now that I could be my little brother's carer. I could earn my way in the family. The good news was that I learned that love and a little importance from my father could be earned. The bad news was that it *had* to be. There was, in my early years, no free gift of love. For I don't think my father had any conception of unconditional love. Had he had such feelings, he would have crushed them, as he crushed all 'soft' sentiments. It was clear to him that his children and his wife should be there to be a credit to him. They were there to follow his instructions and to behave in a way that reflected well upon him in the eyes of other people. So fragile, indeed, was his self-esteem that even the behaviour of young children could damage it. How people judged his worth was of paramount importance to him. Children were one of the many means – like clothes, cars, drinks, and social status – which could cast a rosy light upon him.

The Unhealed Wounded

To write this account of my father is still painful to me, and I feel guilty about exposing him to the public eye. Such things were never talked about in our family. He had many wonderful qualities: generosity, family loyalty, courage, daring, and fortitude. He never complained. He had no pity for others, but he also had no pity for himself. To be at all times without self-pity is a rare virtue. To understand all, is to forgive all. But as a child I did not, could not, understand. And even if I had recognised these admirable human virtues at the age of five, they would not easily have coloured my image of God the father. A God who is a good fellow and fun over fences would not have been a viable concept in the later half of the twentieth century.

After my father's death I discovered a pen wiper and various cards I had made for his birthdays still in his desk. He had kept them for forty years. This was a shock to me, a complete surprise. He had treasured them all that time, through at least five changes of house. He must have loved me, after all. And even as I write that sentence, I feel, still, a feeling of amazement.

I also feel enormous pity for him. Because I am an adult I understand why he behaved as he did. He had lost his 'real mother' (his words, not mine) at the age of five, when his nanny was fired for using the word 'bloody'. His birth mother was far from normal. In her latter years she was so paranoid that she did not dare to walk out of her house into the garden, and she ordered the curtains drawn and the doors all locked from three o'clock onwards. My grandfather, his father, was a bully. He had handed over eight-year-old little Darby to his prep school headmaster with the words: 'This is my son. Beat him well.' My father recalled that as he said these words, Walter Haddon was beating his boots with his riding crop, backing up the verbal threats with physical language. No wonder my father was not a good father. He had not known what it was like to have a kind and loving father so, like many of us, he passed on the only fathering he knew. Like the old proverb, when the fathers have eaten sour grapes, the children's teeth are set on edge.

Worse still, he had been boarded out for a whole term in the care of a housemaster who abused him. A traumatised little boy, himself, he had learned to murder empathy. Yet it did not die completely. Carrying the pain of unhealed wounds, he could not – literally could not – bear the extra pain of others. So he struck out. Anger at other people's weaknesses replaced the pain of fellow feeling, and protected him at the expense of others, including us little children.

In later life, he and I developed a wary friendship. I never told him my troubles, merely related my successes. We swapped amusing gossip or anecdotes, as if we were two friendly acquaintances rather than father and daughter. It worked well, even though it was a very attenuated form of father-daughter relationship. Indeed I was one of the few close family members with whom he had a continuous relationship without a disruptive quarrel. It was a near thing at times, but we succeeded in staying in touch.

The only way that I could stay on good terms with him, however, was to hide my real life from him completely. When I got to University, I set myself free from him. I refused to go out with the young men he considered suitable. I kept my private life secret from him. I never took young men home to stay with him. My first and my second husbands only met him once before my weddings, to neither of which he was invited. He never complained. We never discussed it. He must have been hurt but he never showed it.

I did not cut him out of my life entirely, because I still loved him. I merely cut him out of intimacy, since it seemed, and indeed was, safer that way.

I learned the main lesson of childhood well. Keep quiet. Do what you are told to do, however you may feel about it, and with luck nobody will notice you. Escape authority as soon as possible, for those in authority are unpredictable and likely to be angry. 'The eleventh commandment is never to be found out,' my father pronounced. 'It is the only commandment that really matters.'

The other direct lessons were similar. 'I'll leave my mark on you. You may hate me but you can't escape it,' my father used to say to me as a young child. I used to hate him for saying that. But it was true. From him I learned not to trust. It is folly to trust the unpredictable. Above all, I learned the vital survival lesson of emotional dishonesty. If you don't trust somebody, you don't tell them what is going on. In particular, you do not tell them if you are unhappy or angry. It is not safe to do so, since unhappiness will be met with unkindness and anger with an even greater anger. You pretend everything is all right. Better still, if you can, you pretend to yourself that everything is all right.

I learned good things from my father too. I try harder than most people, because I learned in my childhood that it was possible to earn love. I saw him go through life never complaining and never giving way to self-pity. I saw him relish the enjoyment of good food, good wine and good company. I think of him a lot and hope that I can follow his example in this. I am my father's daughter, not just in my everyday secular life but in my spiritual life too.

CHAPTER TWO

LEARNING
TO LOVE

I learned about love from my mother. How odd it is that, with the exception of an occasional hymn or the writings of Julian of Norwich, God is never compared to a mother. The Father, the Son and the Holy Ghost are all apparently male. In Protestant Christianity there is no female figure at all, for Mary, the mother of God, is usually only mentioned at Christmas time and there is little interest in the women disciples. For those without a father or with a difficult father, the Christian image of the Family of God has little help. In theory the figure of Jesus could be the way out of these difficulties. If God is your Father and is terrifying, then at least Jesus is your friend, the all-loving figure. But somehow I could not see Jesus as my friend. I could only see the suffering Jesus, the martyred near-naked figure, blood pouring down him, wounded in hands and feet and heart. In the church, where I attended Sunday school every week, he was in the stained glass window behind the altar. A victim-God. His death, rather than his life, was the most important thing about him. And he had died for me. If Jesus was the perfect man, I was going to have to be like him. The good life was going to be the life of a victim.

Victimhood is not a good concept on which to base a human life. We all know people whose model of themselves

31

is that of a victim. These are the complainers, the people helpless to help themselves, the permanently unhappy, or disgruntled, the over-sensitive and the manipulators. I am all of these at times and I do not like myself when I am thinking in this way. For victim-thinking is usually negative – why does it happen to me, if only life had not been so unfair, I blame the Government/council/my parents. In this category I do not place the true victims in life. Victim-thinking can create unhappiness where there is really no need for it at all.

If victimhood was the religious life, then there was another victim nearer at hand for me to model myself upon – my mother. She lived for, rather than died for, her children, she declared. She had nothing else in her life, she said, except perhaps her little terrier, Grumpy. She had trained as a painter at the Royal Academy but had given up her painting altogether at the suggestion of her own mother. 'She told me that if my marriage was unhappy, I should give up my painting and concentrate on becoming a proper wife,' she explained.

My mother was alone in the world. Her father died just after my birth, and her mother died when I was about eight. A couple of years later her elder sister died of lung cancer. She had no other relatives because her only uncle broke off contact, after my father had injured his child. My little cousin, whom I do not remember, had come to stay with us on the farm. He had wetted his bed and my father had boxed his ears so severely that he had to be taken to the doctor. Understandably, his parents had not wished to know us after that. Even after she left my father, my mother made no attempt to get in touch with them. She took upon herself the burden of my father's bad behaviour. She bore the shame of his sin.

It was not due to Christianity that she took others' guilt upon herself. She had been brought up in an entirely atheist home. Her parents, both Cambridge dons, had turned their back on the Christianity of their childhood. Her father, who had been remorselessly beaten by his clergyman father and his stepmother, may well have felt that Christianity was a sham. Of the source of her mother's feelings against it I know nothing. Yet these two non-believers brought their daughter up to feel almost continual guilt and shame.

When I think of my mother now, I think of her sadness, a sorrow that I can feel in my own heart with a tightening of the chest. Just as my father's body language was lordly, relaxed and dominant, so hers was apologetic, tense and submissive. She was very thin, pale, and often unhealthy. She walked without grace, and her movements were clumsy. Sometimes I have wondered whether she had a kind of mild spasticity, for she could rarely walk across a room without falling over the furniture, or lay out cutlery without dropping some of it.

She was always poorly dressed. While my father dressed in old clothes for a day on the farm, my mother always dressed in old clothes, whatever the occasion. She wore her clothes till they fell off her. Perhaps the habit had started in war-time, when clothes were rationed. It was maintained throughout her life. At her death, I went through her wardrobe and the only good clothes were the ones I had bought for her. The others were a pitiful selection indeed. She clearly felt so badly about herself that she could not deck herself in good clothes. She was also grubby, wearing her clothes till the dirt was visible on them. This too continued all her life.

She did not share any of my father's pleasures – good food, good wine, or social life. She was excessively anxious about any social occasion, so that for her parties were an ordeal, not a pleasure. She did not ride. Her only attempt to do so had been foiled by the fact that my father put her on a very wild horse, which immediately bolted. She never rode again. I do not think there was any subject upon which both agreed, so that even the pleasures of conversation were denied to them. Mildly malicious gossip, the refuge of the unhappy, was also out of the question since it merely ended up with them taking sides, my mother defending any third party from my father.

She had only her children to live for. We three were not what she had originally wanted from life. She told us so. She would say: 'I did not want to have children, but I have loved you very much since I had you. I am a devoted mother.' It has been said, ' She lives for others and you can tell the others from their haunted look.' Cruel words about an unhappy woman, but in the sting of them there is some truth.

The only times I remember my mother being happy during her marriage, were short periods of stolen time. I have a photograph, taken by me at the age of about ten, of her in a primrose wood. She and I and my little brother, whom she is embracing in the photo, had gone there to see the primroses one afternoon.

I look back and I can still remember the magic of that unusually warm spring day just across the railway lines of a nearby village. I remember the damp moss underneath the coppiced hazel trees, the green dog's mercury and the primroses themselves. It was magic because of their beauty, but also because we three were alone together. She and I knew that this happiness was transient. It could not last. I can look at her in the photograph and see in her eyes the mirror of my own fear. We would have to go home. The kettle must be put on the Aga and everything must be prepared for my father's homecoming.

Other photos show her less relaxed. She is usually badly dressed in well-worn clothes, but in the old black and white photos you cannot see the dirt. She wore long pink bloomers with a further pair of knickers below, true passion killers if there had been any passion left in their marriage to kill. All her clothes were worn so long, that the whites faded into grey, the wool was bobbled, and the cuffs of both blouses and jackets were threadbare. Yet we were one of the half-dozen richest people in the village.

It was a bizarre feature of our lives that while my father had six horses in the stables, two grooms, and a Rolls Royce, we children were also dressed very badly. I was particularly shabby because, as the second girl, I lived entirely in clothes handed down by my sister. My mother created her own shabbiness by wearing clothes that should have been thrown away. 'Good clothes' – and there would only have been two garments at the most, one frock for winter and one for summer – were kept in the cupboard and hardly ever worn.

She looks slightly ill in all the pictures. She was painfully thin for much of her life, so much so that I wonder if she was partly anorexic. She certainly developed a wide range of food fads, refusing to eat onion, garlic, tomato or potato skins, the peel of apples, most kinds of lettuce, chicory, radishes, all herbs except for parsley, parsnips, swedes, turnips, white bread (then, later, wholemeal bread for a change), cream, buttery sauces, curry, or any spices. Later in life she gave up all meat and, just to make things more complicated, would only eat one egg a day. She had a wide variety of minor ailments, including insomnia, lower back pain, irritable bowel syndrome, and constant indigestion. Her inner emotional pain wreaked its revenge on her body. She and I ate bicarbonate of soda remedies most days, topped up with lavish quantities of Dr Collis Browne's remedy for diarrhoea, a concoction which in those days had morphine in it. With a double dose of Dr Collis Browne, life certainly attained, if not a rosy glow, then at least a spaced-out soothing quality.

Living a life of acute unhappiness, she also took barbiturates, the then equivalent of today's tranquillisers. On occasions, with great difficulty and courage, she would wean herself off the pills, only to take them again when life got too painful. I also took them. I was put on barbiturates (I was told by a reliable family friend) somewhere between the age of eight and ten. I was probably given them because she and I were so close. She assumed that I, like her, lived in a state of constant unhappiness and nervous tension, an assumption which made this more likely. It was a mild form, perhaps, of Munchausen's syndrome by proxy. If she was taking barbiturates, so should I. She suffered from ill-heath; so did I. She was a victim; so was I. Our identities sometimes blurred. Towards the last few months of her life, when she was ill with cancer, and heart trouble, and not too clear-headed, she started talking about my heart trouble. In her mind, if she had heart trouble, so did I.

This closeness allowed me to become expert in evaluating her distress. From the age of eight, and until the end of her life, I could tell her exact state of mind within five seconds of her speaking, even if she was just saying 'Hello'. I could chart her emotional pain with astounding accuracy. I was the barometer of her feelings, most of them sad and painful.

Like all her children, I saw her suffer every day. At every meal time, I would watch her take the verbal abuse. We sat at the long oak refectory table with my father at its head. She sat at his left-hand side with my little brother beside her. My sister sat next to him on his right, and I was opposite my brother. The light came in from the garden through the window behind me. It fell on her face, lighting up its misery. My father's eyes, half turning away from the light to focus on her, would glitter as he made an opening cruel remark, designed to wound. She would react to it, first by arguing then perhaps falling into dumb silence. He would increase the tempo with an even crueller tirade. A mulish, obstinate look would come over her face, the only sign that she was angry. Next would be visible signs of her distress. She would, if she spoke, begin to stammer. Her head would begin to shake – with fear, I suppose. And this would produce greater anger from my father. As Stalky, the Kipling boy hero, says: 'The bleating of the kid excites the tiger.' She never cried. I never saw her in tears during these meal times. Indeed, in fifty years I never saw her shed a single tear. She too had learned it was better not to cry.

She was gentle, meek and mild. She was powerless. She was unhappy. Emotional distress simply rolled off her in waves. For the rest of my life, when I was away from her, I would think of her, and her unhappiness would come into my mind. (It still does, even though I am trying to think of her as happy now.) I never thought of her, say, happily walking her dog. I would think of her being lonely, anxious, or sitting at the dinner table with my father shouting at her.

Even when she was apart from him, she found happiness difficult to achieve. She worried about everything. A day out would be prefaced by anxieties about the weather, the food, and the route. She was always apprehensive about what Americans call comfort stops. Journeys were punctuated with frequent stops to find 'somewhere behind a hedge'. Public lavatories worried her, so she preferred fields if possible. All meals were nightmares. If she found items on the menu which did not contain the forbidden foods, she would find the portions too large or too rich. Alcohol, which relaxed others, seemed not to give her any pleasure. A glass of sherry was the most she would allow herself.

She was my protector. I knew she loved me because she told me so. She tried to stand up for me as far as she dared. Mostly she did good by stealth on my behalf. When Moppet, my white cat, caught one of the doves that lived in the farmyard dovecote, my father punished him. He took the feathered corpse, dipped it in paraffin, and tied it round the cat's neck for a whole day. It was my mother, who after several hours of helplessly watching the poor animal's torture, surreptitiously untied the burden and took Moppet away into the spare room where my father would not find him.

Poor Moppet. I cry as I write this. The cruel and pointless punishment broke him utterly. As he tried to lick off the paraffin, he was ravaged by diarrhoea. He had a feline nervous breakdown, and reacted by spraying urine, as cats do. He became shabby with matted fur because he did not groom himself properly. Finally he was run over on the nearby main road. I have a memory, perhaps inaccurate, of my father showing me the body. It seems unlikely that he did this out of kindness.

It is a terrible thing for a child to see animals tortured and in pain. This episode, moreover, was the pattern for family life. We looked on as my mother was verbally tortured daily. My father was all-powerful and frightening. My mother was almost as helpless as us children and always unhappy. Only by surreptitious behaviour, rather in the same way that I would lie or try to avoid notice, could she slightly diminish the effects of his cruelty. Standing up to him was out of the question. She was a victim like us.

Some people will say that this was irrelevant to my spiritual life. I do not think so. It presented me with a clear choice – the powerful assertiveness of the tyrant or the powerless kindness of the victim. Be an abuser or be a victim. If I wanted to be good and kind, I would have to choose to be the victim. Besides, there was a victim-God, immortalised in his pain and suffering, in the stained glass window above the altar. What is more, I was told that the right way to live was to imitate him.

My mother protected me and I protected her. In return I loved her dearly and tried to make up for her unhappiness. If my love could have healed her wounds, I honestly think I would have died for her and, with the single-hearted love of a child, not resented the sacrifice. My mother, after all, had sacrificed her happiness for me. She had given up her painting to be a wife and mother. 'I tried to protect you children,' she would say later on in life. 'I stayed with him until you were all old enough to be in boarding school.' No wonder sacrifice was an idea that I knew about. It spoke to me. During Lent, I gave, not part of my pocket money, but all my pocket money every single week into the blue collecting box of the Society for the Propagation of the Christian Gospel. And I took on the duty of trying to make my mother less unhappy. To make up for my father's harshness to her, I loved her all the more.

Christmas and birthdays were celebrated with home-made presents from us children. My best and most hard-worked creations were made for her. I found many of them in her desk after her death, preserved in the same way that my father had kept my less ambitious offerings. In the anxious time when she took away her possessions from my father's house, in the break-up of their marriage, she had taken all these – hand-painted calendars and cards, wax flowers, and little poems, kitsch human figures made from seaside shells glued together.

The difference in this melancholy discovery, compared with the similar discovery in my father's desk three years earlier, was that their existence did not surprise me. I always knew I was loved by her.

At the beginning of each term, when I went back to boarding school, I left behind me little love notes. 'Don't worry, Mummy. I love you,' one of them read. I was already mothering my mother. My job in the family became to look after my little brother and to look after my mother. I knew she needed love desperately and indeed there was little or none in her marriage. What I didn't realise was that her desperate cravings for love could never be satisfied.

I was also aware that I must try not to worry her or trouble her in any way. It was not that she would be unkind to me if I shared my distress with her. I could, and did, go to her with my troubles and know that she would kiss and hug me. But she would lift the burden off me and take it on herself. She would suffer my pain, on my behalf. If I confided a worry to her, she might say two days later: 'I have worried a lot about your difficulties.' If by this time it was no longer on my mind, I would blame myself for having put her through an anxiety that I no longer felt.

So big was her daily burden of unhappiness, that I felt I must not add to it. She was so sensitised by her existing pain, that I must be always kind and careful. I must spare her, as much as possible, any further distress. I learned I must never be angry with her. She already put up with so much anger from my father, that I must not add to this. If you had asked me: 'Do you ever feel angry at your mother?' I would have answered, 'No. I love her.' Not feeling anger was the sine qua non of love – as I saw it, anyway. Love required the honing and adaptation of self to others' needs. Love meant being no trouble to others. Perhaps I knew this from an early age. 'You were a perfect baby. You never cried,' she told me later. 'You would just lie in your cot and tears would roll silently down your cheeks. And later I could leave you with your toys and you would play for hours without bothering me.'

I dared not be frank with my father about anything. I built walls around my life so that he could not see in. With my mother I could discuss anything and I never hid from her the details of my love life. She met almost all my boyfriends and came to my second wedding. (I asked neither parent to my first wedding. As they refused to meet each other again, it seemed the fairest way to go on.) But out of pity, I could not always be frank about my feelings with her either. I dared not express anger in front of my father, for fear of the pulverising anger that would roll back at me in response. I tried not to express anger to my mother, because of her distress. I could not bear to add to her pain.

So emotional dishonesty or denial was the only way to live. I learned to swallow emotional pain. If I was not angry or upset in the first place, then I would not need to tell either parent about it. This protected me from my father and it protected my mother from me.

I began to understand more about my parents' relationship in my later life. For I found a readiness in myself to bully my mother. Her helplessness seemed to elicit from me a desire to order her about followed by exasperation. She would express her inability to cope. I would make suggestions or offer to do something for her. She never asked for help directly. She did not need to. Once she had expressed her helplessness I would compulsively try to help. But often she did not want my help. The apparent helplessness had been a disguised desire for attention and love. Then, sometimes, I would lose my temper so badly that I sounded for a little while like my father. Very slowly I began to see that, while I was responsible for my own behaviour and regretted it, something about her asked for it.

Seeing her struggling to live through verbal abuse each day of her life with my father, as a child I had only the slightest, most occasional perception that she played her own part in the awful parody of that marriage. As we sat round the dining table, I would see that the conversation was moving into a tricky area. I would watch, as my mother would deliberately bring up a topic which was guaranteed to make my father explode in anger. 'Why can't she see what she is doing?' I would think. Then I would instantly smother that angry thought, with the feelings of pity that she aroused. Of course, she could not see what she was doing. She was my poor helpless mother, a little bird fluttering her wings against the cage, unable to fly free.

It was years and years before I realised the truth, that two people, not just one, often play an active role in an emotional torturer-victim relationship, and that neither can forgo their role. The torturer bears the heavier responsibility for his active cruelty. But the victim can be an accomplice too, unconsciously eliciting the torture that is handed out. For verbal abuse is a form of attention. Kisses and hugs are attention too. But for the needy person abuse may be better than no attention at all.

My mother had been habituated to emotional cruelty from an early age. Just as my father had weird parents, so did she. Her mother, my grandmother, had taken away her dolls. The poor little five-year-old Joyce had wept as these were packed up in a parcel and 'given to the poor'. She recalled in later years that she had been heart-broken at their loss and had worried that her favourite doll would be unhappy in a poverty-stricken home. A collection of toy soldiers and a fort had been given to Joyce and her sister in their place – a piece of cruel feminism. Her father had been just as odd. Once, when my mother killed her guinea pig by mistake, he had condemned her publicly as a murderer, over the family dinner table. Both she and her older sister were whipped for serious misdemeanours and made to kiss the rod afterwards. My grandfather may have been an atheist, but he had clung to that particularly horrible bit of child humiliation from the Old Testament about sparing the rod only to spoil the child.

Her parents argued ceaselessly. My mother claimed that they loved each other, but acknowledged that their rows were so frequent as to make family holidays seriously upsetting. The parental warfare seemed to create warfare between the two sisters. Her older sister Nancy would truss up Joyce, and leave her tied up in the dark in a box room. In adolescence worse was to come. She suffered from severe acne so her mother, a pioneer in the exploration of radium, took her for radiation treatment, then thought to be some sort of cure-all. Such a high dose was used that all her hair fell out. Her mother, genuinely misguided in her choice of radiation, then showed her cruelty by refusing to let her daughter wear a wig. Joyce had to go to teenage parties bald. Little wonder, therefore, that social occasions were subsequently always an ordeal for her. (The radiation, incidentally, did not permanently cure the acne, and sixty years later it produced the cancer that killed her.)

So serious was her childhood trauma that she had a nervous breakdown in her teenage years. With the loyalty of an abused child, my mother refused to blame her parents for their treatment of her. She, unlike I, never betrayed them by thought or word. She idolised them. The victim in her had been ready and waiting before the arrival of my father.

My mother told me a story which seemed to me to make it clear how little her parents had supported her. Three days before her wedding to my father, she went to her mother and said she no longer wished to marry him. 'You can't stop now. We've arranged everything,' said her mother. This might have been an excusable remark if theirs had been a big wedding. It was not. They married in a registry office in 1939, just after the outbreak of war, with no wedding reception and with only parents in attendance. But the point about this anecdote is not just her mother's lack of kindness. It also highlights my mother's victimhood. If the marriage had proceeded against my mother's own wishes, it meant she was not fully responsible even for her own marriage. Even in this she was the passive wounded.

Like other hurt souls, her need for love and approval, or attention, however abusive, was desperate. She could not get enough of it. In later life, when I was having therapy I began to listen to our patterns of speech. After leaving my father, my mother had taken up painting and become a good painter. One day I said to her: 'I really like that painting of the beehive.' 'Do you, really?' she said.

'Yes, I do. I particularly like the doves in the foreground there.' 'I was worried whether it was up to standard. Do you think it is?' 'Yes, it is one of your best.' 'I'm not sure if I like it. Do you think it's really all right?' 'Yes, I do think so. It's a smashing painting.'

'I thought perhaps that I had got the perspective wrong in the right-hand corner.'

'No, the perspective is fine. It's a lovely painting.' 'I was worried about it. Do you think it's good enough to show?'

And so it went on. The hunger for approval and reassurance was not, could not, be sated. Whatever I said, was not going to be enough. She needed more. And more. Ironically, the persistence in asking for more would make me want to say something rude and childish like 'I think it's a lousy painting.'

Victims truly suffer, but victimhood has one attractive pay-off for the victim. She or he does not have to take responsibility for what is happening. They view the world through essentially passive eyes. Their actions are caused by other people's unkindness. As the passive recipient of hurt, the victim is the 'good' person. It is not their fault. Their good qualities are shown up and enhanced by the horrible vices of the abuser. They can feel good about themselves. Moreover, pity, compassion, and sometimes real help, will often be forthcoming from outsiders. Victimhood, even when authentic in origin, can be used as a manipulative ploy to get sympathy. Just as abuse is better than no attention at all, so sympathy, while less pleasant than love, is at least a substitute for it.

In my childhood I gave her all the sympathy I could manage. I learned that my mother's unhappiness could be soothed by my comforting words. I was useful. I could literally magic away her pain for a bit. The trick was to focus all my attention on her, listen wholeheartedly, and find ways of giving her approval and love. In her later life, my phone calls would consist of my listening for twenty minutes, and talking for perhaps two or three.

Yet I owe my mother very much. My life would have been intolerable without her. To her I owe my capacity to love and to pity others. Admittedly I am sometimes not sure of the difference, but I am glad that I did not have to murder empathy like my father did. My mother's need for love taught me the giving, if not the taking, of love – a gift I am still grateful for. She had great courage. Eventually she stopped being a full-time victim. After twenty-two years of marriage, she walked out. It was a blow from which neither she nor my father ever quite recovered, even though both were happier apart. Both felt lifelong shame about their divorce, a shame made worse by the fact that it could never be discussed. Neither would have contemplated therapy, Christian confession in depth, or intimate conversations with friends, and so the shame that was unexpressed remained unhealed.

My father, who remarried happily, dropped his role as emotional torturer with his new wife. He seemed to have put aside the shame, but it was still there. Very occasionally he would admit to it, if I was alone with him. My mother took up her painting again successfully, but she lived with a deep inner loneliness. She writhed with the reproach of being a divorced woman. Her courage and persistence in the face of despair helped her take a job as a teacher and build a new life for herself. But, like him, she bore the heavy burden of disgrace till the end of her life, a burden unmitigated by her success as a painter or the love of her children.

She left her mark on me, just as my father did. She gave me the ability to love others, to pity others, and to comfort others. She taught me gentleness to others. Her helplessness made me into a helper, rather than a victim. But I also learned to confuse love with pity, to feel that I must always help, that I must never hurt anybody. I could love others but I do not think she taught me to love myself. She could not have done so for she did not love herself. This too left its mark on my spiritual life. For what is Christianity about if not love?

CHAPTER THREE

MILD, OBEDIENT,
GOOD AS HE

We know relatively little about the carpenter's son from Nazareth, but we know for sure that he loved and valued children. He didn't think of children as little nuisances, to be kept out of the way of adults. Nor did he consider them sinful beings who must be taught, trained, constrained and licked into shape by adults. He didn't even think of them as imperfect grown-ups: he thought that adults were imperfect children. He didn't tell adults to teach children: he told them to learn from them.

His words are worth looking at. 'Verily I say unto you, except ye be converted, and become as little children, ye shall not enter into the kingdom of heaven. Whosoever therefore shall humble himself as this little child, the same is greatest in the kingdom of heaven.' In the revised version of the Bible the words 'be converted' are changed to the simple 'turn.' For what is conversion but a turning away from something old, towards something new and better.

Some Christian writers (not as many as one might think) have taken this passage seriously. 'It is not only in a careless reliance upon divine providence that we are to become little children, or in the feebleness and shortness of our anger, and the simplicity of our passions,' wrote Thomas Traherne. 'We must disrobe ourselves of all false colours, and unclothe our souls of evil habits; all our thoughts must be infant-like and clear, the powers of our soul free from the leaven of this world, and disentangled from men's conceits and customs.'

When I was a child the idea that I had a special value just because I was a child would have amazed me. Perhaps I need to pause here and point out that giving a child a feeling of intrinsic value is not quite the same as giving it love. A man can love his dog, but be quite clear that the dog is an inferior being. My father loved his children (though it was difficult, perhaps impossible, for us to see that), but he did not normally treat us as if we had any importance. We were one up from his dogs, true, but certainly nowhere near his level. My mother dearly loved me, but she didn't value girl children or indeed adult women. She disliked and despised them. 'I much prefer men,' she would declare. 'Women are so boring.' It was perhaps the only issue in which she agreed with my father, for whom reproduction was primarily important only in the male line.

By the time I started attending Sunday school at the age of five, I had already absorbed this essentially unChristian message that children existed for the sake of their parents, childishness was without worth, and that girl children, in particular, were of no value at all. Nothing in my early Christian education led me to question this.

I was a 'good' child, if good means being quiet, obeying rules, being no trouble to my parents, and being fond of my little brother. I did not feel good inside though: I felt I was a sinner well before I fully understood the idea of sin. Just as St Augustine (surely a tormented individual, however severely saintly at the end of his life) recalled feeling jealous of his foster brother at the breast, so my earliest memory is of bad, not good, behaviour. I am a toddler, sitting on my pot in the nursery and I take off one of my shoes. I throw it away, possibly out of the window. What I recall about the episode is not a joyous feeling of throwing something in the air or even the pleasures of rebellion. I remember simply that the action was very wicked. St Augustine sees his earliest memory as proof of original sin. Was I already a child of sin? In the eyes of my father, seeing me as a cuckoo in the nest, perhaps I was. Did I feel it even then?

If so, I cannot attribute my feelings of sinfulness to formal Christianity. It predated my proper Christian education. Neither parent was a churchgoer, though my mother was friendly with the vicar of the isolated village of Marston Trussell in Leicestershire where I lived till the age of four. ('He was a bloody old drunk, always in our kitchen,' recalled my father, who had had to share night firewatching duties with him in the Home Guard trench, to the great irritation of both of them.) I was to receive no formal religious education until the age of five, when I was sent to a Church of England school, St Helen and St Katherine's, in Abingdon and simultaneously started Sunday school in the Oxfordshire village to which we had moved.

I think it could be said that my formal religious education came too late to do much good. For there is both formal and informal Christian education, the latter being much more influential than the former. Indeed, it is not going too far to say that there are two kinds of Christianity itself – formal and folk. The latter, folk Christianity, has a power and influence far more powerful than sermons, scripture classes or Sunday schools. For we will learn about religion first from our parents, not the church. My agnostic mother, for reasons I cannot even guess at, taught me to pray. My first prayer was 'God bless Mummy and Daddy, and make me a good girl. Amen.'

I certainly didn't understand the prayer. It was my grandmother on my father's side, a Christian believer of a glum and eccentric temperament who insisted on being called 'Mimi' by us rather than 'Granny', who discovered the extent of my misunderstanding. I went to stay on my own with her in a vast, gloomy Edwardian mansion in Kent. The rooms were full of dark and costly mahogany furniture felled at huge expense from the rapidly diminishing tropical forests. Almost every room had a life-size marble statue of a woman, with a name like Truth or Psyche, intriguingly naked under revealing marble gauze. The house was also a sort of animal mausoleum with dead horses' hooves made into inkwells, stuffed heads of shot or hunted animals on the wall, and mummified elephants' feet made into waste paper baskets.

One night I was invited to say my prayers at the side of her bed. The occasion is still vivid in my mind, for my grandmother was at her dressing table wearing a night gown. A light above the mirror shone on her as she let down her hair. In day time she wore it in plaits ringed round her head. That evening it cascaded in a long grey waterfall right down her back below her waist. As she brushed it with a hundred long slow brush-strokes, like a young girl preparing for her bridegroom, I knelt by the side of her bed. 'God bless Mummy and Daddy, and make me a good girl, and bless Our Men who work for us,' I intoned. 'Our men who work for us' was my version of 'Amen.' Nobody had told me what 'Amen' meant, so I had given it the best meaning I could find. To this day I am not sure what its literal meaning is. I suppose I think of it either as a kind of verbal full stop or a sort of 'Hear, hear.'

My grandmother, however, picked up on my linguistic misunderstanding and made much of it. Her conversation, mostly melancholy remarks about who was dead or dying, was enlivened only by small, pointless anecdotes about children. My first prayer became one of her favoured stories, woven into the dreary monologue which used to put my father to sleep during his dutiful visits.

When I look more closely at that first prayer, however, it appals me. There really isn't anything about it which suggests a loving relationship between me and God. True, he is going to bless Mummy and Daddy, but not me, little Celia. As far as I am concerned, there will be no blessings. He is going to make me a good girl, which automatically suggests that I am not one already. This is not a God who will greet me with heavenly kisses and hugs. This is a schoolteacher God or worse, standing by to make sure I do the right thing.

Later, I still asked for blessings on the men who worked for us, since they were low paid and I felt they needed all the help they could get. I identified with the underdog. I merely added the meaningless 'Amen' in its correct place after it. After all, I truly loved some of the men who worked on the farm. There was Big John who called me 'Angel face', Willie who gave me rides on the tractor, Charlie and Wilf the cowmen who were always kind to me. They gave me some of the fathering that I needed. I felt safe around most of them, as long as my father was not nearby.

I used to soften the prayer further. I would usually pray for blessings on all the family animals by name, one by one – Dinah the labrador, Finnegan the Irish water spaniel, Grumpy my mother's terrier, Moppet my poor cat, Simpkin his white mother and feline matriarch, and Scrappy, the white frightened youngest female. Sometimes I added the fourteen horses, among them the hunters Hailstorm, Thunder, the Galloping Major, Titus Oates, Mrs Robinson, the ponies Bracelet, Mercury and Jute, and the two cart horses Bally and Blossom.

Some of the cats and dogs would usually be lying on the bed already, as I prayed for them. Occasionally there would be the two big dogs and all three cats, each carefully segregated in a separate part of the bed to prevent territorial disagreements. These were my friends and equals. They showered the blessings of unconditional love on me, and gave me comfort in the dark. Kneeling down to pray at the side of the bed was something of an ordeal because I was always frightened that there was something horrid under the bed. Sometimes I could persuade one of the large dogs to sit beside me while I prayed, to guard me. In general, I was frightened of the dark, so the period between the light going out and sleep was an ordeal without their presence.

Apart from that first prayer, I absorbed other messages about God from my environment. Folk Christianity is quite different from the real thing. 'Don't do that. God won't love you if you are a bad girl,' said Mrs Winter as she washed up in the kitchen. No doubt I was being difficult and getting in the way, but such are the doubtful ways children are taught about God. These informal 'lessons' are far more important to most children than the formal sessions in church.

If God Is My Father, How Can He Love Me?

The idea that Christianity is primarily a way of making people behave is a common one. It always has been. Social control – making sure the lower classes don't get above themselves, keeping women and children in their proper place, stopping rowdiness, and reducing occasions for illicit sexual intercourse – is a major function of religion in many people's minds. (I am today amused by newspaper editorials, often written by journalists well grounded in the more enjoyable social sins, sternly demanding that the Church take up its role as disciplinarian to the unruly or the poor.) I suppose that the Ten Commandments are a guide to a stable society, but onlookers forget that they belong to the Old Testament, which was reinterpreted by the New Testament of love. 'I must keep my hands from picking and stealing,' said the dour old Church of England catechism. But this is not the spiritual side of religion, only the moral and social rules of what was in my childhood still a Christian culture.

Even formal Christianity contains a lot of folk Christianity. 'Gentle Jesus, meek and mild,' is what many children are taught about the strange young Galilean rabbi who ended up on the Cross. In the words of the carol, 'Once in Royal David's city', they are told that:

'Christian children all must be,

Mild, obedient, good as he.'

This is social control again and a message quite different from that of the New Testament. The child Jesus, 'our childhood's pattern' according to the hymn, may have been 'little, weak and helpless' and 'dear and gentle', but he grows up to be a twelve-year-old boy who goes missing for three days in order to sit among the doctors in the temple. He gives his parents a terrible fright. What is more, he does not apologise. 'His mother said unto him, Son, why hast thou thus dealt with us? behold, thy father and I have sought thee sorrowing. And he said unto them, How is it that ye sought me? wist ye not that I must be about my Father's business?'

Had I behaved like he did, my father would have given me hours of verbal abuse, partly out of fear and partly for making him look stupid in front of the other pilgrims. My mother in her gentle voice would have upbraided me for her fear and anxiety on my behalf, rather like Mary. But I would have felt full of guilt and shame. There is no suggestion at all that Jesus of Galilee felt any such emotions. He appears to have had considerable self-confidence at an early age. Mary and Joseph must have been good parents.

Of my formal religious training in Sunday school I have reasonably happy memories. We went there on Sunday afternoons, about twenty or thirty of us girls and boys from the village. (My elder sister was tormented by boys pulling her plaits. Luckily, I had short hair.) Sunday school consisted mainly of being told the various Christian narratives and praying the usual prayers of sorry, thank-you and please. I can't remember ever feeling that God was a source of strength or love or comfort, merely that he was somebody to whom you must behave in a particularly polite way. The vicar, Father Goodchild, was a gentle bachelor, very friendly with my unhappy mother. He knew his ministry was to the unhappy and the lonely in the village, rather than merely the respectable churchgoers. He must have perceived that something was wrong between me and God and did his best to change my religious landscape. 'God is not a policeman, Celia,' he said several times. Perhaps he even knew that the relationship between human and God is bound to be based on relationships in this world. But I suppose he could hardly have said, 'God is not your father. He's much kinder and less frightening.' What on earth would have happened if I had gone home and blurted this out? It is the measure of my father's total unpredictability that I cannot be sure whether there would have been a wrathful explosion, or just a laugh.

Books were the other way I learned about Christianity. My favourite book was *Donkey's Glory*. It told the story of Jesus through the eyes of donkeys – the donkey who carried Mary to Bethlehem, and the donkey on which Jesus rode into Jerusalem on Palm Sunday. This was the story of a man who was kind to these humble animals, perhaps the same Jesus who as a child in the apocryphal gospels made birds out of clay, and then set them free to soar into the air. As I grew up I identified closely with the animals who, like me, were under my father's authority, so this book appealed to me greatly. I could love, with spontaneous enthusiasm rather than dutiful obedience, a Jesus who was kind to donkeys. I still love these gentle beasts.

Like other children I took part in the nativity play. I was an angel, reading from the pulpit, chosen because I was a good reader at an early age and also probably because I spoke what was then known as the Queen's English. Christmas Christianity was and is, still, my favourite season of God. I loved the crib, that inspired suggestion by St Francis of Assisi, which made the Christmas story into a kind of dolls' tea party. There were the animals, taking their part in adoring the baby. I would have liked to put my teddy near the crèche, had I been allowed. (If I ran a parish church I would have blessing services for teddy bears and dolls, those child comforters who do so much spiritual good in the world.)

Easter day too was jolly. We had a model of the tomb, surrounded by moss in which primroses were inserted with their stalks in small jars below the moss. Like all miniature scenes it entranced me. The vicar, Father Goodchild, must I think have had a childlike touch about him.

But Good Friday was different. It was quite horrifying. Mine was the generation before television, so we were not immune to the horror of corpses. We did not see that steady diet of death and violence on the small screen every evening. We came unprepared to the Christian story of betrayal, pain, anguish, torture and a terrible death.

From somewhere, perhaps from the hymn 'O sacred head, sore wounded,' that medieval devotional prayer translated into a hymn in the seventeenth century, I got the idea that it was my sins that had nailed Christ to the Cross. I felt I had to share in the blame for his death.

I do not think Father Goodchild can possibly have told me that I was responsible for Christ's pain in the crucifixion. I do not know where the idea came from, unless it was from hymns like this:

> 'Thy grief and bitter passion
> Were all for sinners' gain;
> Mine, mine was the transgression,
> But thine the deadly pain.'

This strikes me as a pernicious doctrine, inculcating immense guilt and self-reproach in the young, unless accompanied by a great deal of careful theological explanation. As a small child, I was not able to see that this was literally untrue, that none of my childish misdemeanours could possibly have had such an appalling consequence.

By the age of eight I had acquired a vigorous and torturing conscience. I knew that I was sinful. I remember one night that I went to bed with guilt on my soul. I had lied, as I often did, to escape my father's anger. But this time I lay in bed and the feeling of shame and guilt burned in me. It was not that I was going to be found out. It was merely the pain of having lied. I then braced myself to go downstairs and confess in tears to my mother.

I also felt guilty that we were among the wealthy inhabitants of the village. In this small world, we were at the top, and I did not know of the larger world in which we occupied a less elevated rank. We had all the exterior signs of riches – land, domestic help in the house, a dozen or so outside employees, large meals, private education, horses. I had a pony of my own, of which I was frightened, and I hated riding. Nevertheless, I knew that I was very very lucky and I felt ashamed of disliking what most little girls yearned for. I don't think there were children without shoes in the village in the 1950s, but there was a clear distinction in schooling, food and housing between us and them. This gulf was made greater by the way I was taught to speak differently and told off if I pronounced words with a Berkshire accent. Other differences were that I was forbidden to read comics or to go to films. I was dressed differently too. At one of the few village children's parties I was allowed to attend, many of the children had pink frocks, or dresses with lots of net layers. I was, as always, wearing arty green silk. 'So good with your eyes,' said my mother. 'You would look sallow in pink. Besides, all that net is common.' I yearned for pink net.

I was allowed to play with some, but not all, of the 'village children', so in Sunday school the presence of a wider selection of children added to my anxiety. My mother had carefully explained that because we were richer than them, it was particularly important not to be stuck-up. Distinctions were to be preserved, of course, but it was incumbent upon me to be particularly kind and nice to them, and pretend that the differences didn't exist. Above all, I was not to swank. I must always be polite to less well-off children. One of my severest punishments was for being rude and showing off in front of the foreman's daughter. I had said to her, 'My father owns this farm. Your father is only a worker here.'

Relationships with the women who worked in the house were complicated too. There were two daily women and a series of cooks who came in to make lunch and cakes for tea. My favourite was Mrs Percival, a cockney evacuee from London who had stayed on after the war ended. She was terrific fun and would occasionally say, 'I wish I could be away from this weather on a South Sea island.' With laborious care I drew for her a picture of her wearing a grass skirt (and some form of garment covering her breasts) surrounded by naked savages, also in grass skirts. She was their queen. This drawing pleased Mrs Percival no end, and she chortled at the skimpy clothing. My mother, on the other hand, warned me about the dangers of being cheeky and disrespectful. Real ladies – which the daily women could never be – had to be careful in their position always to be sensitive. To be unkind was one of the worst sins and the ideal was not to hurt anybody, ever. Because I was so lucky at being well-off, I must be particular in this matter. Drawing pictures of Mrs Percival almost in the nude was not respectful.

I don't think either my father or my mother felt guilty about being well-off. They took it for granted and felt at ease about it. I'm not sure they even fully appreciated their good luck. I definitely felt uncomfortable from an early age. The story of the rich man and the eye of the needle haunted me. It seemed to me then, as it still does, that Christianity requires the rich to give away their worldly wealth. Yet most of us don't do it. Frankly I dare not. And I do not remember this dilemma ever being discussed either during my religious education or in later life. For me, it is the skeleton in the cupboard, the deep dark hole of silence in Christianity. Even when I gave away all my pocket money during Lent, not keeping back even the price of a sherbet lemon, I knew it was not enough.

What was enough? As a child I kept trying. Even at a young age I could see there were many opportunities for sin. Being good and kind and not talking back was clearly a start. Not lying, which I often did out of fear. Being generous to others. Not taking the largest slice of cake. That was also a social obligation, carefully explained by my mother. This in particular impaired the pleasure of tea with the Miss Joneses, two unmarried daughters of a former vicar rather similar to Cranford ladies. They had exceptionally lovely cakes which sat on a circular many-tiered stand, each on a beautiful, lacey paper doily. I would dutifully take the smallest piece and wish I didn't have to. But being good required restraint, self-control, and sacrifice, which naturally impaired any spontaneous delight. There was nothing about being good which suggested enjoyment was anything other than a somewhat dangerous irrelevance.

Doing something that hurt me was being good too. The more it hurt me, the better it was. This involved eating things I disliked. I can still recall a particularly loathsome cake, known in those politically incorrect days as a nigger's head, offered to me by the Miss Joneses. It was brown, round, and scattered with brown decorative chips of the kind known as hundreds and thousands. Inside was a vile-tasting dark cream. I ate it all, because good girls ate things they hated. It was unkind to refuse food in somebody else's house, and therefore a sin. Somewhere I found a story about a saint who drank up all the pus and dirty water, after cleaning a wound. This was the highest example of goodness about food. (I occasionally ate cow dung, but that was different. I did it to show off in front of other children.)

There were many other hateful foods I had to eat in our own house but luckily I did not have such a strong sense of sin about my difficulties at home. Family meals, always the occasion for arguments between the parents, were made more stressful by the fact that I hated Brussels sprouts, cabbage, fish skin, parsnips, turnips, all forms of fat, bacon, soft eggs, and the skin and bones in sardines. All these things could sometimes be swallowed with a drink of water, but would occasionally make me vomit with disgust. Unlike the saint, I could not be sure I could keep them down.

We children were made to eat them all. 'Waste not, want not, that I might live to say, Oh how I wish I had that crust which once I threw away,' my father would say, mimicking the words of his own nanny. Luckily, the family dogs came to our aid. Lurking under the refectory table, they would help us with everything except cabbage and Brussels sprouts. 'You're a sardine skinner' my father would sneer as I carefully took out the backbone and cut off the fish skin. Once he made me sit in the nursery in disgrace with a congealing piece of steamed fish in front of me, until I ate it. My mother came to my rescue and took the fish away quietly once he had left the house. She too had been tormented by being made to eat up every piece of food on her plate, and in her case there had been no kind mother to rescue her. Uneaten meals would simply appear at the next meal until eaten. No wonder she had developed food fads in later life rather than simple enjoyment of food.

What else was evil? Losing your temper and shouting was wrong for women, not for men. 'A low and gentle voice is an excellent thing in a woman,' my father would say. 'You're screaming like a fishwife.' I already knew that anger was bad. Anger meant shouting, threatening, sneering, and saying hurtful things. It hurt other people badly. I could see the horrible effect of my father's anger every single mealtime. I knew how much it hurt me and how much it hurt my poor mother. So I must not feel anger.

All this was part of my Christian education – the folk part, not the formal part. I absorbed the lessons well. Religion was about being good, doing what people told you to, not doing wrong things or unpleasant things. Goodness was restraint, self-denial, self-sacrifice, obeying rules, being no trouble, being nice, not being angry, feeling guilt, refraining from action, and being polite in all circumstances. The love, spontaneous enjoyment, self-outpouring, gratitude, forgiveness, letting go, and straightforward anger (think of the moneylenders in the Temple) which are also to be found in the life of that Galilean rabbi, were missing. If somebody had pointed them out to me, and I do not recall that anybody did, I'm not sure I could have taken them in anyway. I had the gentle Jesus meek and mild version firmly fixed in my mind. It now strikes me as pretty far from the real thing.

Some readers may think I have wandered from the point in this book by describing my spiritual life in terms of my father and mother. At the heart of Christianity, to my mind, is not a story of a god come to earth. Many religions have had variations of the descent of a god. Most religions have a god or gods, who are the subject of ritual praise, who may grant requests, and may even forgive sins. But our own Christian God's descent is meant to offer us a loving relationship.

Nobody can understand the human-God bond outside their own cultural background. We learn about relationships from seeing them around us, and for most of us that means seeing a mother and father figure. Their relationship is bound to be our model, bound to set the whole tone of our thoughts about loving and being loved. Theologians will no doubt be able to set me right on this matter and many others. They can solve the intellectual puzzles of Christianity to their own satisfaction, perhaps even to mine. But I have learned, rather late, that life is not a puzzle to be solved and that for me the spiritual life is not an intellectual matter at all. My heart has its own life which must be understood, or perhaps merely better experienced, by appeals to feeling not intellect.

If God Is My Father, How Can He Love Me?

Did anyone ever tell me that God loved me, no matter what I did or who I was? If they did, I didn't hear it. Perhaps I could not. For something far worse than ordinary Folk Christianity had happened to me. I had learned that I was doomed to hell, fated to suffer the bitter pains of burning in eternal fire. Through no fault of my own, I was an outcast from God's mercy. Hell, not heaven, lay about me in my infancy.

CHAPTER FOUR

THE EVERLASTING
FIRES

A few minutes in one's lifetime can cast a deep shadow upon a whole spiritual journey. For me this dark inner place came from a woman, whose name I do not even remember. She was an elderly Irish woman, plump, wearing a nanny's uniform in grey, stretched tight over the bust with a nurse's watch hanging from her left-hand breast pocket. On her head was, as I recall, some sort of nanny's head-dress. She had been hired to look after my little brother, when my mother came home from the maternity hospital. She was, I think, a Catholic, though I am not sure how I knew this. My little brother's arrival in the family was a time of great rejoicing for my father and mother. At last they had the boy they had always wanted. My sister and I were turned out of the second best bedroom, which we had shared. I was put into an adjoining small dressing room next door, while my poor sister was banished into the outer darkness of a tiny room down a long corridor. Even the sizes of the rooms, let alone their position in the house, made clear the relative importance of us three children. Seniority, that hierarchy of age so vital to children, counted for nothing compared with gender.

My brother was a noisy baby, crying out with the full power of his little lungs. In his first few weeks of life he was installed, not in his large bedroom, but with the nanny in the biggest spare bedroom. Meals were taken up to her there. She slept in the room with him at night, so that my mother could have uninterrupted sleep. Such a distance between mother and baby was no great matter in those days. The guru of baby care was Truby King, author of many manuals, who recommended that children should never be spontaneously picked up. They were expected to lie silently in their cots in the periods between a rigid schedule of feeding and burping. We three children spent hours lying in a pram in the garden, totally ignored by all adults. This was not neglect, far from it. It was the correct way to rear babies in the 1950s. Mothers had to suppress their natural feelings of wanting to pick up a baby, in order to achieve the right kind of detachment from a crying child.

Did I welcome that little brother in the year of 1951? I hope I did. I knew that he was welcomed by my father and mother. He was the answer to my father's prayer, prayed on his behalf by me that morning by the side of the bed containing my pregnant mother. He was what they wanted. He was also a large, healthy and pretty baby with blonde hair. I don't remember feeling jealous. I paid homage to, rather than resented, his important status as the son and heir. The idea of 'daughter and heiress' had not occurred to me. I loved him. My situation was made no worse by his arrival, since I was not my father's favourite anyway. I had no status to lose.

I would go and look at him in his cot in the spare room and I would talk to the nanny there. The spare room was an odd place, very cold and very formal. It had only one small gas fire to heat it for we had no central heating in those days, and only one rather small window to light it. But the beds were huge Edwardian affairs, high off the ground, and made up with bolsters as well as pillows, with very stiffly starched sheets and pillow cases decorated with hand embroidery. It was a formal room decorated to impress guests and I remember feeling awe, and perhaps a little dismay, as I went in. I dare say that the nanny, stranded in this rather gloomy room, was pleased to have somebody to talk to, even if it was only a five-year-old child.

Somehow in the course of these conversations and baby worship, the question of baptism arose. Perhaps the nanny was wondering why my brother was not christened or why there were no plans for this. A church christening was still the social norm in those days, but my parents had not conformed. Neither my sister, nor I, had been baptised, even though we were attending a church school run by Anglican nuns. In retrospect, I wonder if they would have allowed us in as pupils, had they known. In those days even Church of England nuns wore full-length robes with proper wimples. They were imposing but, as I remember, kind. I was not frightened of them and I loved Sister Alethea, my favourite nun, who ran the infant class. She can have had no idea that I was a little pagan.

Until I met this nanny, I think that I too was ignorant of my unchristened state. After our conversation I must have asked my parents about it and then found out that I had never had the benefit of baptism. They would have thought little of it, but my heathen status clearly shocked the nanny. As a good Catholic she felt it was very wrong. Perhaps it was with some idea of influencing my parents through me, that she told me what it meant.

'If you die, you will burn in hell forever,' she said. 'It is only by baptism that you can be forgiven your sins by God.'

I was horrified. 'What about my little brother?' I asked. 'Will he burn in hell forever too?' 'Sure, he will not. He is a dear little innocent. He will go to limbo. That's the place for little babies. He is not old enough to have sinned,' she explained. 'But you are a big girl. You have sinned. You cannot to go limbo with him. You will go to hell.'

I already knew that I was sinful so I had no reason to think she was wrong. Yet the unfairness of this was bitter to me even as she spoke. Was there, I begged her, no escape from this awful punishment?

'I could save you,' she volunteered. 'If I saw you dying, I could make the sign of the cross on your forehead and say the words, 'In the name of the Father and of the Son and of the Holy Ghost.' It should properly be holy water, she explained, and done by a proper priest. But if I was on the point of death, God would accept ordinary puddle water and a lay person with the essential words. My father could do it, for instance.

This was little comfort to me, because I was absolutely certain that my father would do nothing of the kind. He would just laugh at the idea. He was virulently anti-God. I pictured myself lying dying in the middle of the farmyard, a small puddle of water fit for my salvation just nearby. Nobody would do it. I imagined adults crossing the yard and failing to pause to help me. Or if they did stop to help, they would call a doctor. Nobody would think of calling a priest or of making the sign of the cross. My father wouldn't. My mother wouldn't either. They wouldn't even know the right words.

None of the men on the farm would do it, unless I was well enough to ask them, and I probably wouldn't be if I was dying. Even Willie, the Irish Catholic and one of my favourites, wouldn't do it because he wouldn't know that I needed it. I should lie there dying, doomed to eternal fiery flames for the want of a drop of that puddle water so close but so useless without the right words and gestures.

Perhaps the nanny spoke of some of the terrifying Bible verses, for hell in the New Testament is even worse than hell in the Old. It is the New Testament, based on the covenant of love between man and God, which seems to glory in the details of torture. 'But the fearful, and unbelieving, and the abominable, and murderers, and whoremongers, and sorcerers, and idolaters, and all liars, shall have their part in the lake which burneth with fire and brimstone: which is the second death,' says Revelation. She must have echoed some of this in her talk, because I was haunted by the idea of the flames.

I was doomed to be there among the wicked through this terrible omission of the correct ceremony. It was particularly painful to me that my little brother was safe from this awful doom. He was, after all, my replacement, the baby they had wanted me to be, the son they had always planned. In this world he had an importance that I would never have. In the next he had the chance, if not of heaven, at least of a safe limbo, whatever that was. For me there lay ahead only hell, the visible expression of a God's judgment on me – that God from whose love and mercy I was forever banished by my failure to be baptised.

I did not tell my parents of my fears. By the age of five I had learned not to confide my difficulties to my father (if I ever had done so). My mother was spending a lot of time in bed resting and I did not tell her either. Perhaps I knew I must not trouble her while she was still recovering from childbirth. Nor could I tell my older sister, because she and I were not close. I suspect that even at that early age, I had learned to try to keep my sorrows to myself.

The memory of my despair and utter terror stays with me almost half a century later. Did that middle-aged Irish woman have a particular power of expression which made her words so convincing? Or was it that I knew already that I was of no importance? Was I, the unwanted child staring at the wanted child, particularly vulnerable to that horrifying message?

Had I been a true pagan, the full implications might have escaped me, but I already knew about hell. How I don't know, but know it I did. I suspect the very idea of hell is so shocking to most children, that once they learn about it they will never forget it. They may not believe in the literal existence of hell, but the idea of it will never entirely leave them.

Perhaps I had already heard some of the gospel stories that mention hell. There is the tale of Lazarus and the rich man. The afterlife is going to even up the score, so that the unfeeling wealthy in life will suffer eternally after death. Abraham says, 'Son, remember that thou in thy lifetime receivedst thy good things, and likewise Lazarus evil things: but now he is comforted, and thou art tormented.' What is more, Abraham refuses to warn the rich man's five brothers about their eventual fate. This is the good news gospel for the poor, but not for the rich. The unfairness of a lifetime is going to be reversed into eternity with no let-up. The parable has a relish in his come-uppance. If I had heard this story in Sunday school, I would have known we were among the rich. Worse still is St Matthew's gospel with its parable of the sheep and the goats. Those who have failed to exercise charity are dismissed to eternal punishment with these words: 'Depart from me, ye cursed, into everlasting fire, prepared for the devil and his angels.' Then there are the final words of St Mark's gospel, 'He that believeth and is baptised shall be saved; but he that believeth not shall be damned.'

By now I was having a religious education at St Helen and St Katherine's. I knew about Jesus, for instance. In the infants' class we used to sing a little hymn which started, 'I do belong to Jesus.' Sister Alethea, who would accompany us on the piano, had explained to us that we were His children and that we belonged to Him because we had been christened.

When I realised I hadn't been baptised after all, I understood that this mattered a great deal. I stopped singing out loud. To sing 'I do belong to Jesus' would be a lie. I, alone of all the class, did not belong to Jesus. I did not dare to continue singing, yet I did not dare to stop. So I merely mouthed the words silently, hoping that nobody would notice my shame. For a time I succeeded with this deception, but all the rest of my schooling now went for nothing. The brightly coloured diagrams, showing how well we had progressed in learning, was now a mockery. I had been proud that the pink cut-out rabbit with my name was at the top of the tables tree, outpacing the green rabbit belonging to Duncan, my rival. Being top at tables was not enough. I was doomed.

I remember days and days of this unhappiness, knowing that I was outcast and unworthy. We had a little shrine in each classroom, tended by the children with flowers and candles. I played my part, but in trepidation. I was not worthy. I dare say that there were only a few days of this misery but they seemed very long. It is no small matter for a child to believe that hell gapes without remission.

Sister Alethea was my saviour. Not that I told her, or asked for her help. She noticed I was no longer singing out loud. 'Why aren't you singing with the others, Celia?' she asked.

'I don't belong to Jesus.' I told her and the tears flowed as I explained why. At last I could unload the heavy burden of fear that I was carrying. She proved worthy of my confidence and took up the matter with my parents. Some weeks later baptism was arranged, thanks to her intervention. The vicar became my godfather. My godmother was a family 'friend', whom everybody in the family, myself included, hated. Sister Alethea sent me a religious card which I kept for years and may even still have among my documents. I was saved from hell. I knew I owed her a great deal, and indeed I still think I do.

For those who feel the troubles of the young are not to be taken seriously, this could be just another whimsical anecdote about children. My gloomy grandmother could no doubt have incorporated it into one of her monologues, as a nice little story about a little girl who found herself in need of saving. She would have thought it funny and sentimentalised about it. But in my life it has cast a long shadow.

My christening, instigated by the loving Sister Alethea, was probably the only action that could end the fear and turmoil I was experiencing. She was right to insist on it and, if prayers of gratitude reach those in heaven, may mine reach her. She was a loving figure in my life.

But the damage was not to be entirely healed. Hell still loomed with a horrid force in my mind, even if now I knew that I was saved from its inevitability. God's inexorable cruelty towards the unchristened – those kept in eternal torture, with their sins forever unforgiven – passed unchallenged by adults during this episode. Indeed, the fact that my baptism was so rapidly arranged reinforced the idea of its urgency. It were well done quickly, so that I should not lie dying in the farmyard, cut off from all salvation. Did anybody try to explain it all to me? Did anybody say that God wouldn't do such a terrible thing to a small child? Did anybody tell me that I wasn't a terrible sinner, only saved from hell by the font? Did they say that God, particularly Jesus, loved little children without requiring them to be especially good or even to be baptised? If they did, I do not remember it. I suspect that they did not know how much I had suffered. They may even have found my dilemma rather funny. The emotional sufferings of small children are often underestimated, ignored, or simply discounted as being of no importance since children are not yet 'reasonable' beings.

If I look back at that experience with the ignorant but perhaps well-meaning Irish nanny, I would classify it as serious spiritual abuse. Just as the sexual abuse of small children can ruin their sexual behaviour for a lifetime, so spiritual abuse has the same potential for lifelong harm. In some ways I have never recovered from those days of believing I was doomed to eternal torture.

The idea that in some way I am hopelessly outcast has

never really left me. Throughout my life I have felt that I do not truly belong. I have felt like an outsider. Some of this probably comes from the old family label, 'the cuckoo in the nest'. Some comes from knowledge of being, from my birth onwards, surplus to requirement. But much of it comes, I think, from this episode when I discovered I was not like the other children, that I alone was barred from redemption and God's love.

If you were to ask me what I really believe in, not with my rational mind, but deep down in my heart, I would admit that I still believe in a God that condemns me to hell with only slight hope of forgiveness. The loving God, the forgiving Jesus, and empowering Holy Ghost – these I find difficult to believe in. They do not come naturally to my belief like that shockingly cruel God does. This is the God that looked on to those in torment who suffer 'in the presence of the holy angels, and in the presence of the Lamb.'

Naturally, my rational mind is repelled by him and I do my best not to believe in him. I turn from him. I know that it is bad for my happiness to believe in him. I know that this hellish God will drive me to dangerous attempts to block him out altogether or to equally dangerous despair. But he is still there, patient, baffling and powerful, ready to come back into those parts of my mind that reason cannot reach.

No wonder that some years later I cut God out of my life entirely. I did not love Him. Why should I? He was infinitely more frightening than my father on earth, whom I already feared, and infinitely more powerful. Salvation, loving kindness, forgiveness, grace, these were the froth on the surface of religion. Underneath was the reality of Hell.

CHAPTER FIVE

A DAMNABLE
DOCTRINE

John Milton, the puritan poet of the seventeenth century, would be horrified to know that, in an indirect way, one of his great epic poems triggered my rebellion against God. His conscious aim when he wrote 'Paradise Lost' was 'to justify the ways of God to man'. But as numerous critics have pointed out, these great poems have what we nowadays call a hidden agenda. As a sixteen-year-old I studied them for my 'A' levels and they were the final straw that broke my attachment to Christianity.

'Paradise Lost' deals with the rebellion of the angels and the fall of man. 'Milton was of the Devil's party though he did not know it,' wrote William Blake, that strange visionary who lived a century or so after Milton. For the most sympathetic hero of Paradise Lost is not God, but Satan. Rebelling against God, he flies to Paradise, where he tempts Eve to pick the forbidden apple. In her turn she hands it to Adam who, to please her, takes it. Their disobedience prompts God to turn them out of Paradise. His punishment for their sin brings death. It also brings all the ills of ordinary life, not only on them, but on their descendants for all time. I had, of course, already come across this great myth of the fall of man and the concept of mankind's original sinfulness. The two slightly differing versions in Genesis had been read to me in Church and it had been explained that the faithful did not have to believe these were literally true. A well-educated little girl, I had read a book about fossils and evolution by the age of about ten, so I knew how mankind had ascended from apes. (In those days the tree of life showed invertebrates at the bottom and man right at the top, the living triumph of an equally mythical progress!) So it was not just the story of God's savage punishment for the small sin of scrumping apples, or even for the larger sin of disobedient curiosity, which made me decide to turn away from Him.

Up to the age of eleven I had been a serious Christian churchgoer. At Sunday school we were given a coloured stamp by the vicar to put into a little book, to show that we had turned up. On those Sundays when I could not go, usually because my parents had arranged some other event, I was given a stamp anyway. But I grieved and worried about my absence. I don't think I loved God, though I may have felt some kind of sympathetic love for Jesus. (The Holy Ghost was for me, as it is for many children, a mysterious and fairly unpleasant figure. I was frightened of ghosts, though this one was meant to be a benign one.) I loved something about Church, though I am not sure what it was. Father William Goodchild, the vicar, certainly played his part. Perhaps I took after my mother, whose emotional needs brought out the caring side of vicars. I was not frightened of him and I definitely liked him. What is more, I felt he liked me, for which I was grateful, though I felt slightly guilty in case it was just because I was not one of the village children.

The church itself was a delight. Light slanted in from the plain windows on the right-hand side, undimmed by stained glass. The choir stalls and lectern had been carved by a previous vicar, who must have spent his life's work translating his faith into wood. Those were the days when vicars lived among their parishioners for decades, sometimes even for a working lifetime.

The font was for me the place where I had been saved from the inevitability of Hell. And opposite the church entrance was the table where the Christmas crib and the Easter tomb were placed. There was also the collecting box for the S.P.C.K. somewhere near the hymn books. Some spiritual echo from my early years in Sunday school never left me even in my most atheist years. I have loved churches, preferably old ones, all my life and I have felt they were a refuge, even during the years when I was definitely an enemy of Christianity. Even the tacky evidences of worship, the bad-taste plaster statues, grimy poor paintings, and over-elaborate flower arrangements are dear to me. I felt safe in churches and I still feel safe there. I suspect in my youth I may have felt safer in church than I did, at times, at home. To love old churches may not be to love God, yet it is to love a small aspect of him. Perhaps the empty space of churches holds a tiny trace of his presence, like the lingering scent of a person who has left the room.

More religious, and distinctly less spiritual, education was to follow when I arrived at my girls' boarding school, a Christian foundation with the motto 'Quietness and Strength', strange and amoral characteristics that I do not think I have ever possessed in the slightest. I liked most of the teaching staff, except for the woman who gave us scripture lessons. On what my dislike was based I do not know. I do know that our religious education was a series of lessons based on the Bible. Bits of the Old Testament such as the death of Jezebel were wonderfully bloody and awful, but on the whole most of it seemed very boring indeed. Nobody suggested that there was beautiful poetry in the King James' version of the Old Testament. The thundering justification of God in the book of St Job, which convinces by its poetry rather than its argument, was ignored. Perhaps my teacher thought it might raise unease about the morality of God.

When I look back at those lessons, I do not remember any discussion of the status or origin of the Bible. If it was the word of God, what did we mean by that phrase? We knew that Elisha succeeded Elijah and we even knew that he sent bears to eat up the little children who had mocked his baldness – 'And he turned back, and looked on them, and cursed them in the name of the LORD. And there came forth two she bears out of the wood, and tare forty and two children of them.' But we never discussed the appalling immorality of the prophet's reaction. Does God really punish so viciously little children who mock baldies? Is this the word of God? If so, what kind of God is he? The various Old Testament stories were simply laid before us, data to be absorbed without thought and without criticism.

Did we 'do' the Gospels? If we did, I remember nothing much. Discrepancies and variations, which to my mind make the stories intellectually interesting even to a non-believer, were passed over. So was the theology of this remarkable story. Perhaps the school, practising a kind of institutional denial, thought that by ignoring all the difficulties, they could keep our faith intact from intellectual doubt. Denial, which I have practised in my own life, is, of course, the emotionally and intellectually dishonest way of coping.

Maybe the school just wanted an easy life and thought that any questioning of Christianity might bring the parents down upon their back. The historicity of Jesus was also never mentioned so that I was able, when I turned from God, to dismiss him as a completely invented figure. Looking into the matter later I was surprised to find that the historical evidence for the existence of this young rabbi from Galilee is not much questioned. The evidence for his existence is, like that of Alexander the Great (another god on earth), well documented, even if Jesus's status is only divine to believing Christians.

My interest, weakened by boredom, was finally terminated by the voyages of St Paul. There they were on the blackboard – a chalk trail wandering round the Mediterranean. Who cared exactly where he went? Why did it matter? I took a dislike to St Paul then because it was all so dull. It was as if anything interesting about the stories was immediately lost. St Paul's anxieties for the new Church, his disagreements with Peter, the sheer strain of outwitting the authorities – we learned it by rote, as if where he landed was more important than what he experienced. Everything was presented without excitement, without doubts, without interest.

Of the matter of our souls there was no talk at all in those lessons. If the theory of Christianity is true, the well-being of our souls here and in the hereafter is perhaps the most important issue of our lives. We did not discuss it. The great question of salvation, the question which has both empowered and tortured Christians through the ages, remained ignored. Both heaven and hell, as ultimate destinations for eternity, were equally passed over. It was as if this Christian foundation was only interested in pushing into us the various stories of the Bible. We knew that Joshua succeeded Moses, but we did not know that God might work in our lives.

Nobody was interested in what we might feel about what we were reading. I think it was the Quaker George Fox who said, 'The Bible sayest this, but what sayest thou?' We little girls spent quite a lot of time surreptitiously searching the Old Testament for the dirty bits about sex – circumcision, the sin of Onan, Noah's drunken behaviour, some of the wilder bits of Leviticus, and so forth. That was the most gripping part of my scripture lessons.

Of course, there was chapel. We came to morning chapel every weekday, after a short period on the playing field, and without any chance to wash in between. The morning incense that arose from our worship was the smell of healthy girl sweat. But the hymns were fine and it didn't last very long. I think I quite enjoyed it. It was certainly preferable to the muddy lacrosse or cricket practice which had preceded it.

On Sundays we attended matins and evensong and, for the older girls who had been confirmed, early morning communion. In those days parishes in the Church of England did not expect all the worshippers to take holy communion each week. Matins and evening prayer, both beautiful services by Thomas Cranmer, were the weekly ritual – a ritual tossed away in the reformation of the Prayer Book. '1662 Evensong is the best reason I know for belonging to the Church of England,' says a friend of mine. I love it still. Thomas Cranmer's gentle version of the Catholic Compline, with its dying fall, moves me more than any other service. Evensong acknowledges that the devices and desires of our hearts may be hurtful to us, and that God can lighten our darkness when we are suffering the perils and dangers of the night of the soul. For me it holds back the inner darkness and its tone, if not its words, seems to understand the miseries which we humans can inflict upon ourselves and others.

Sung evensong in the school chapel was not the only spiritual blessing of that school. The other was Father Mo, as we called Canon Mowbray Smith, the school chaplain. If God is love, then in my eyes then and now Father Mo was a good expression of that love. He was a portly man, dressed in grey shirt and trousers, and always wearing a clerical collar. A bachelor, he lived in a messy flat at the top of the playing field. It was foggy with pipe dust and full of old books. He was very keen on cricket and it can only have been because of him that I was, on one occasion only, chosen for the school's Under Fifteen Cricket Team. I was last man in and was never bowled out, due to the fact that Father Mo grossly cheated as umpire and failed to call the LBW.

He was a simple man, perhaps even a simpleton, a source of irritation to some of the staff. I am not sure if he was stupid but he was certainly a fool. I hope God keeps a special place in His heart for all fools like him. Wherever Father Mo went, he had toffees in his pocket. 'Have a toffee? They're not fattening,' he would say. As he ate the inadequate and unpleasant school meals with us, he may have known that most of us were always hungry. We were only allowed a small quantity of sweets a week, and we were forbidden to acquire any extra food under pain of punishment. So a single toffee was a great luxury.

Proof of his loving nature lay in the summer strawberry treats. Every summer term, Father Mo would motor down to East Anglia from Berkshire to collect strawberries and cream for the whole school. As his car was small, this took at least eight journeys, journeys that must have been about four hours there and four back, possibly more. He paid for the strawberries and cream out of his own pocket and this lengthy pilgrimage probably reflected the fact that somewhere in East Anglia (he came from Hunstanton in Norfolk) he could get them wholesale. To schoolgirls on an enforced diet of gristly stew with mashed swedes or carrots and lumpy potatoes, strawberries and cream were the highlight of the summer term. This extravagant gesture by the school chaplain was undertaken, I believe, simply to make us happy. It was a foolish act of kindness.

His hospitality included inviting all the sixth form to Sunday supper in twos or threes throughout the year. Supper was baked beans and sausages (from the same Heinz tin) heated up over his tiny gas cooker, with as much buttered toast as we wanted. We ate with him in front of the sputtering gas fire. This was high gastronomy for us, far better than the usual Sunday supper of one small triangle of processed cheese, an apple, and bread and margarine. Sometimes there was not even enough bread for a third slice. As I write this, it sounds as if I must have been horribly greedy. I wasn't. I was just hungry.

Forty years later I weep at the memory of those toffees, strawberries and baked beans with sausages and the toast dripping with butter. If somebody now asked me about the simplest insight I have ever had into the love of God, I would point to Father Mo. He loved me, I know. I still feel a passionate gratitude towards him for that. Yet my sister just found him boring and remembers how the school used to cough through his sermons alphabetically – one cough for the first word starting with 'A', the next cough for 'B' and so on. Father Mo meant nothing in her life.

Some people play a special part in our lives. Their influence is powerful, though they may never know it. When Father Mo died about fifteen years later, I was in the fullest expression of my distance from God. Yet he was, though dead, to play a significant part at a turning point in my life. But for him, the moment when I turned away from slow self-destruction, back towards a better life, might never have happened. He spoke to me from beyond the grave in a way that I will describe later.

So how did my rebellion against God start? Many young women and men have lived through boring scripture lessons without losing their faith. Why did I lose mine? Why did I turn to the devices and desires of my own heart? I did not simply lose my way. I deliberately decided to turn against that way, that truth and that life.

The process of disengagement from God began with confirmation. We had to fill in a form saying whether we would, would not, or might, be confirmed. My elder sister, braver and less conformist than I was, had in her time refused altogether to go through the process. I ticked the option that I 'might' be confirmed, always the coward's choice. There must already have been a series of doubts growing inside me. But I dealt with doubts, as I had dealt with other difficulties, by denying that they were there. Doubts might upset Father Mo, you see. Upsetting people I loved was something good girls like me didn't do. To be good was to be no trouble to others.

The preparation for confirmation swept me along quite nicely. We learned the catechism by heart. I remember still that a sacrament is 'an outward visible sign of an inward spiritual grace', one of Cranmer's beautifully balanced phrases. I was also given private confession by Father Mo, before the great day – an occasion which allowed me, with his help, to get rid of some guilt which had plagued me since the age of seven. Like the confession later to be found by me in therapy, it relieved the burden.

I worked myself up into a state of quite convincing holiness, marred only by my irritation when my parents refused to buy me a special white dress for the confirmation ceremony. I, like some of the others, had to borrow a much-washed one from the school. I felt, before, during and after the ceremony, especially holy and rather smug about it. Then, the very next day, I broke out in the rash of scarlet fever and was isolated in the school sanatorium, with no hope of going home for the holidays till it was over. My smug holiness evaporated instantly. My reaction was simply that God had played me a dirty trick. Was this what I got for doing the right thing? If so, all this religion stuff wasn't worth bothering about. So I stopped believing. It was never the same again.

The falling away from God was surprisingly easy. I continued to take part in the school's religious ceremonies, including communion. Not taking communion would have invited comment and (I thought) possibly punishment from the school authorities. And it would have upset Father Mo. So I did what I had always done, kept my head down, told nobody, and went through the motions. Some enjoyments remained – hymn singing in the school choir, reading the lesson, and borrowing the occasional religious book from Father Mo. The whole question of the salvation of my soul seemed simply to have slipped away, leaving behind it no guilt, sorrow, or concern. I was eased of all that potential discomfort and worry without even thinking much about it.

Then, in the next school year came the deliberate intellectual turning-away. A different matter to the easy lapse. It was, as I have said, the time when I was studying the fourth book of John Milton's epic poem, 'Paradise Lost'. One of the books of criticism I read about it was called 'Milton's God' by William Empson, a poet and critic. This examined the nature and motives of Milton's God. Empson wrote: 'It is always a puzzle, in trying to follow the mind of a Christian, to estimate how near the surface of his mind or his judgement is the basic evil of the system he has submitted to.'

This, my first exposure to theology, shocked me, as I believe it would shock any loving, reasonably normal person. Man's fall had been the result of disobedience. By taking the apple Eve, and with her Adam, had been cast out of Paradise and doomed to a world of death, disease and sin. And, because of them, all their descendants had been doomed too. The poet describes the ills which would now befall humanity:

'All maladies
Of ghastly spasm, or racking torture, qualms
Of heart-sick agony, all feverous kinds,
Convulsions, epilepsies, fierce catarrhs,
Intestine stone and ulcer, colic pangs,
Demoniac phrency, moping melancholy,
And moon-struck madness, pining atrophy,
Marasmus, and wide wasting pestilence,
Dropsies, and asthmas, and joint-racking rheums.'

The same God punishes the snakes. Even John Milton seems to acknowledge this is unfair because Satan himself took the form of a serpent, something which presumably the snakes in Paradise could do nothing about. Nevertheless God curses them in 'Paradise Lost', just as he does in the Bible, in another piece of almighty unfairness, this time to animals.

> 'Upon thy belly grovelling thou shalt go,
>   And dust thou shalt eat all the days of thy life.'

To say the least, this kind of behaviour does not suggest a kind God. As Randolph Churchill said, returning a Bible he had been lent and had read thoroughly during war time, 'Isn't God a shit?' Worse still, just because Adam and Eve have fallen, all are doomed to sin. This is the idea of original sin, that there is within all of us an inherent tendency towards evil. True enough, one might feel. But there is a further bite to the doctrine. All those who are sinful will go to hell, that place of eternal torment. The fall of Adam and Eve dooms them and all humanity to pain in this world and possibly everlasting pain in the next. But how can individuals deserve this, if by their nature they are predisposed to sin?

Christianity, even in the gloomy seventeenth century, is supposed to offer a new relationship between God and human beings. The merciful solution, that God highlights in the poem, is to send his Son to earth. God enters history to rescue us from the punishment of God. If you look at it from the point of view of Jesus Christ, this seems at first sight all right. He loves humankind so much that he gives up his life.

But why is it necessary? John Milton, seeking to justify the ways of God to humanity, explains it in the third book of 'Paradise Lost':

> 'Man disobeying
> Disloyal breaks his fealty, and sins
> Against the high supremacy of Heaven...
> He with his whole posterity must die;
> Die he or justice must: unless for him
> Some other able, and as willing, pay
> The rigid satisfaction, death for death.'

When I read this, I realised this was not just a quirk of a seventeenth-century poem. The whole of Christianity was full of blood sacrifice metaphors. Jesus was the Lamb of God, not because lambs are innocent lovely little creatures, but because they are killed on the altar at Passover. Even the communion service mentions the death of Jesus Christ as 'a full perfect and sufficient sacrifice for the sins of the whole world'. It is there in the text, as clear as anything each Sunday.

I knew that the story of Adam and Eve was just a myth, so God couldn't be blamed for putting a tempting apple tree in Paradise and then waiting to see how people will respond to it. Yet the theology, so horribly outlined by John Milton, still presented me with an impossible God. The doctrine of original sin was still with us. It was the explanation and justification for the death of Jesus Christ. Human beings have fallen from grace and can only be redeemed by Jesus Christ. Without him, we would go to hell.

I suppose I could simply have just denied the doctrine of

original sin, but even this would still have left me with an unacceptable God. For Jesus to save us, we must (for some reason) need saving. Even if there is some reason other than original sin for our sinfulness, we still need the intervention of Jesus. And the price of our salvation was hours of torture and a slow lingering death for the Galilean rabbi. This disgusting death was apparently what would satisfy the blood lust of the Eternal Judge, Maker of All Things, God the Father. Either he was powerless to save humanity any other way, or he was a rigid personality, requiring blood for blood, unable simply to stretch out his hand in mercy. What kind of God was this?

A father who sacrifices not himself, but his son, is himself repellent. No loving father would do this. My father would not have done this. No half-way rational judge would sentence children to everlasting hell just for the sins of the ancestors. What kind of person wants to see blood to satisfy justice? By the 1960s even those who believed in capital punishment argued it was necessary as a deterrent, not as some kind of abstract payment of justice. Even in the Old Testament story of Abraham and Isaac, the death of Abraham's son is not required at the hands of his father – 'And Abraham lifted up his eyes, and looked, and behold behind him a ram caught in a thicket by his horns: and Abraham went and took the ram, and offered *him* up for a burnt offering in the stead of his son.' The God of Genesis seems to have required blood, but at least not human blood.

Why should the New Testament God require the death of his own son? It's an abhorrent thought even if one could argue that the God who required the blood sacrifice was also the God who was paying it. It remains a piece of punitive thinking unworthy of a God. Or so I thought then, and still think now.

There was worse to come. For the first time I came across the idea that all unmerited suffering (including that of children and animals) is in some way the 'participation of the creature in the sinless offering of Christ, and is offered in Him and by Him for the sins of the whole world'. This idea is meant to make undeserved suffering more acceptable (What about deserved suffering? Why should that somehow be OK?). But, as Empson commented, it merely meant that God could enjoy their suffering as well.

The more I read, and I read my way through the school library, the more I discovered other authors who rebelled as I did. 'I can indeed hardly see how anyone ought to wish Christianity to be true; for if so the plain language of the text seems to show that the men who do not believe, and this would include my father, brother, and almost all my best friends, will be everlastingly punished. And this is a damnable doctrine,' wrote Charles Darwin in his autobiography. The poet Shelley remarked that no man of honour could go to heaven because the more he reverenced the son who endured, the more he must execrate the Father who was satisfied by his pain. The visionary William Blake, making notes for a book, wrote: 'What is the Will of God we are ordered to obey?... Let us consider whose Will it is... It is the Will of our Maker... It is finally the Will of Him, who is uncontrollably powerful... So you see that God is just such a Tyrant as Augustus Caesar...'

Perhaps a happy, loved sixteen-year-old would have been able to shrug off all this unhappy theology as merely a religious mystery. But I was a sixteen-year-old who already, at some deep childhood level, believed in the God who condemned five-year-olds to eternal torment through no fault of their own. I believed in a frightening, abusive God, who required his children to do what he wanted, an absolute God whose rigidity was only tempered by his unpredictability. Empson's book suddenly put these deep childish beliefs into words. It pointed out the moment in 'Paradise Lost' when Belial, one of the devils, calls God a torturer. I looked at this God, this God that already had imprinted himself in my heart, and I turned away from him. Who wouldn't?

Milton's theology, which is still the official theology of some Christian churches, fitted my deepest fears and feelings. It expressed these horrors in a convincing belief system. There was nobody to turn to for advice. There was nothing in the Christian foundation of my girls' school where these feelings could be expressed. Father Mo, loving as he was, was no intellectual and, as I have said, I did not want to hurt him anyway. Besides, he had left the school in my last year when I became seriously interested in Empson's book. There was no school counsellor in those days. My godfather had moved away to Cornwall and I never saw him again. My godmother was somebody everybody disliked, somebody I saw only once or twice after the baptism, and somebody I would never have thought of confiding in. My parents were non-believers. By now we had moved to a different village and no longer even knew the local vicar. A braver person than I might have tried to raise this important matter with the school authorities. But I was the family wimp, the coward who tried to stay unnoticed, and whose duty it was to make sure others, rather than myself, were kept happy.

The solution was to turn away from this poisonous God

of fear and horror. I began to develop a phobic reaction to spirituality. I wanted none of it. My life henceforth would consist of body and mind. I would treat the soul or inner spirit as non-existent. I hated and feared it, with its power to instigate guilt and punish with hell. Perhaps if I turned from God, I could be relieved from guilt and shame. Religion was a set of rules, designed to take the joy out of life. The very word God made me angry.

I thought I had left it all behind me. But turning away from is not the same as letting go. Not thinking about it helped, of course. Denying it was part of me helped, too. It was helpful to resolutely forget that God which somehow lived in my unconscious mind – and to run away from him. These precautions required vigilance. Just as I was for years careful not to let my real father know any of my troubles, so I was careful to reduce all contact with God or the godly.

I was spiritually wounded and thought that by hiding from the cause of that wound I might heal myself. I could build walls to keep my real father out of my intimate life and I could build walls to keep my heavenly Father out of it too. But would the walls hold? And what would they cost me?

CHAPTER SIX

THE DEVICES AND DESIRES
OF MY OWN HEART

Living without God was at first like stepping out into the light. I was seventeen and full of excitement about my mental prowess. I had won a place at Cambridge University, one of a small number of women who made up less than a tenth of the students there. I put my faith in my own efforts. Neither religion nor politics now interested me, but I was grateful to my own intellect which had sprung the family trap for me.

At last I would soon be able to leave my mother and father, whose pain and anger were at a peak during their unhappy divorce process. I was setting out for a new life. I would put behind me the evils of a repellent ideology, the pain of my mother, the anger of my father, my own low status as a mere girl, the world of foxhunting bores and desirable rich marriages for women. I was going to walk into the brave new world of what seemed to be the equality of the intellectual life. Not for me the superstitious ceremonies of an outmoded religion. Not for me the restrictive rules of an old world. Everything that I hated seemed all of one piece – God, my parents' awful marriage, and the rules of socially acceptable behaviour.

Christianity seemed to typify the world I was leaving behind, a world where women knew their place, which was primarily in the kitchen or behind a vacuum cleaner.

Women knew their place in church too, which was to keep silent, as St Paul had advised. 'And if they will learn any thing, let them ask their husbands at home: for it is a shame for women to speak in the church.' The same saint had laid down that men were definitely the rulers, women the ruled, within marriage. 'Wives, submit yourselves unto your own husbands, as unto the Lord.' Nobody in my Christian girls' school questioned this or even thought it worthy of comment. No wonder I hadn't much enjoyed St Paul's voyages round the Mediterranean, carrying the message that women must be subordinate to men.

In Milton's epic, too, I had found what used to be the official Christian position. Eve, still un-fallen, says to Adam:

'My author and disposer, what thou bidd'st
Unargued I obey; so God ordains.
God is thy law, thou mine: to know no more
Is woman's happiest knowledge, and her praise.'

If this was the Christian position, I did not want to be a Christian.

From a very early age I knew I wanted a different life from what was then the conventional female one. I was not a feminist by conviction, just a woman who wanted out of the female trap. I dreamed of being a scientist and, because all scientists were men, I imagined myself as a bearded man in a laboratory. I don't think I knew even one married career woman during the whole of my childhood. The only women I knew who worked were domestic cleaners or cooks and teachers. The former, true, were married but who wants to be a cleaner? The latter were all single. They were spinsters, despised for having failed to get a man. For them a career was second best, or so it was generally thought. At my girls' boarding school we assumed (possibly quite wrongly) that the unmarried women teachers hadn't even had sex. They probably hadn't even been kissed. Ever.

Perhaps if I had grown up in a happy marriage, the dilemma of having to choose between marriage and a career would not have seemed so terrible. The 1950s world of housewives and mothers does not seem so unattractive to me, now that I am older and perhaps a little tired. Women who lived in that world had the chance to pursue their hobbies and enjoy a relaxed social life. There was no pressure to earn money or to succeed in a career. At its best it was a life of cultured leisure in which a woman ruled the home and brought up her family. I had visited the home of my best friend and seen one happy couple. What was noticeable was that the woman was not just a helpless victim in the relationship. She seemed to exert considerable power and influence over her husband and over their life together.

But what I had seen most of the time at home was the life of a married victim, and what I hadn't seen with my own eyes my mother had told me anyway. She was a woman forced into painful sex by a brutal husband; bullied mercilessly every single day of her life; reduced to a dependent childlike being; a woman who could not enjoy the leisure and money that she had, who was terrified of social occasions, and who seemed to have no enjoyable hobbies. It was difficult to think of a single area of her life in which she was happy and fulfilled, except perhaps in her relationship to her little terrier, Grumpy. In all other areas, she seemed to be, and indeed declared herself to be, pitiable.

Before her marriage, my mother had been a good painter, but afterwards gave up painting completely. 'I gave it up for you children,' she explained. It was marriage and children which had trapped her into a life of misery and destroyed her talent. Her own mother, my maternal grandmother, had advised her that since her marriage was unhappy, she should concentrate on being a full-time wife. Indeed, there was a female tradition of sacrificing talent in my mother's family. My grandmother, a pioneering student at Cambridge whose doctorate was given by Dublin university since Cambridge refused them to women in those days, had given up all her serious studies when she married. This was not an inevitable choice. Her own women's college, Newnham College, had started life with a married woman as its first principal. My grandmother, in the absence of serious study, however, had settled for Sunday painting, amateur composing, a little light poetry, flirting with her husband's male students, and publishing one amusing travel book. My father, who hated his mother-in-law, always claimed that in return for her sacrifice she had made her professor-husband's life hell. 'He was the toad beneath the harrow, who knows where every tooth print goes,' said my father, quoting Charles Kingsley.

My mother had thus been brought up in a household where women knowingly settled for sacrificing talent in exchange for social conformity. Her elder sister had stopped any kind of work, even though her marriage was childless. My mother followed that model. Trapped in a terrible marriage, she threw away the only area of her life, her painting, which could have given her some happiness. It was, incidentally, a sacrifice which my father had never demanded and I suspect that she gave it up out of anger, hurting herself because she did not dare hurt him. The sacrifice was in vain. She eventually found living in her wasteland of a marriage too much to be borne. About the time that I turned my back on God, she had run away from my father. With enormous courage and persistence, this hitherto helpless, childlike woman struck out on her own. She found herself somewhere to live, took up painting again and gained a divorce on the grounds of my father's mental cruelty, one of the legal categories which in those days ended a marriage. But the cost was lifelong shame, a shame so extreme that she felt it to the last year of her life.

Neither of them wholly recovered from the failure of their marriage. My father's shame at the very idea of divorce equalled hers. He too had been brought up to think that divorce put both man and woman beyond the social pale. In desperation during some of their final rows, he offered my mother a comfortable life living apart, separated, even legally separated, but not divorced. Anything but divorce was his idea. She refused this.

During this uncomfortable period in their lives, while they were living apart but not yet legally divorced, I continued spending time with both of them. I was told that since I was over sixteen I could choose whether I wanted to see both parents. But I dared not make the choice. I was like one of the monkeys brought up by cruel experimenters to have artificial parents who blew jets of painfully hot air on them. Far from leaving these parents, the abused monkeys clung even harder to them. Because I had not been well fathered, I needed my father. I did my duty, visiting him regularly. There was love there too, on both sides.

Both parents were beside themselves: my mother with anxiety, hidden shame and rage, my father with open shame and rage. At the time I felt pity only for my mother, who faced a future which was uncertain in the extreme. I was wholly on her side. Today I look back and I am sorry for both of them. I see also now, as I did not see then, that my father behaved with great financial generosity and restraint. He settled a substantial amount of money on the mother of his children even though he did not want her to leave him. He did his best. He even tried to be a good father to me. I have a pathetic letter from him, in which he mentions that he will try to look after us children. He asks that I should remind him if I need dental appointments or new clothes, because he had not been used to taking responsibility for these. Perhaps, had he been a different sort of man and had I been less of the rebellious adolescent, their separation might have brought him closer to me.

As it was, their estrangement plunged me into turmoil. In those days there were very few children of divorced couples at my boarding school. Indeed, I did not know of a single one. My parents' break-up was the outward visible sign to me of their inward adult failings. I did not want to be like them, either of them. They symbolised everything I did not want for myself. I turned from them both and from the fatherhood of God at the same time. I also was clear in my own mind that I didn't want to be a woman and, as I couldn't do anything about it, I should just have to try to behave like a man.

Then there was sex. As I then saw it, Christianity forbade sex outside marriage and also decreed that marriage, however horrible, must be endured for life. Christianity appeared to value sexual frustration well above sexual fulfilment. Doing it was bad. Not doing it was good. Yet again God was a spoilsport. When I look back, I wonder where this certainty about the Christian position came from. I don't remember ever listening to a sermon about sexual matters. I'm quite sure that the scripture lessons didn't include anything about it – the subject would have been far too exciting for us girls to forget. We had had a class about 'the facts of life' when we were nearly twelve. The chemistry mistress, Miss Fredericks, naturally known as Freddy, had drawn diagrams of the male and female sex organs on the blackboard for us and taken us conscientiously through each stage, from penetration onwards. Freddy, a survivor from a Japanese prison camp, was a somewhat eccentric teacher, both witty and frightening, but with total command of the class. We eleven-year-olds dared not even giggle as she ran through the mechanics of sex.

My mother did not discuss sex with me till I was thirteen. She was driving me back to my boarding school and in the course of the drive she said to me, 'Do you know the facts of life?' Embarrassed, I assured her that I did. Of course she had taught me a lot about sex already without meaning to. I had absorbed from her that sex within marriage was associated with pain, both physical and emotional. She was the living proof, the evident victim, of sex without tenderness, fun or love.

Other than that, I do not recollect any guidance whatsoever from anybody about sex. In the echoing silence that surrounded the subject, most of us girls picked up the notion that sex was wonderfully exciting and desirable but A Bad Thing Except In Marriage. Religion endorsed this, except that even marriage was only second best. Best was virginity. Somehow in my mind Christianity had become all about Not Having Sex.

I dreamed of excitement and romance, not the chilly calm of virginity. Many nights I would look out of the window of the school dormitory, count seven stars, and make a not very edifying wish – for a boyfriend with a car. My dreams were the simple ones of a kind found in Mills and Boon, or Harlequin romances. I would pray for romance too, to a God who disapproved of sex. This God allowed it only within marriage, and marriage, of course, had doomed my mother almost to a lifetime's unhappiness. So if you were going to have Christian sex at all, you were likely to pay for it with the prison regime of marriage. In fact, the core of folk Christianity seemed to centre around sexual rules. Hurtful gossip, self-satisfaction, selfishness, unkindness – did I ever hear these condemned by Christians? Sex, on the other hand, was definitely bad, even unforgivable. In those days divorced people, particularly the 'guilty' partners (and one had to be guilty for the divorce to take legal effect), were quite often forbidden communion in the Church of England. In a village where a large proportion of inhabitants still went to church, this was noticeable.

My father did not make up for my mother's shortcomings in sexual guidance. His attitude to sex and women was as unpredictable as every other area in his life. When I was caught kissing a boy after dark on the school cricket field, he just thought it funny. Yet he would intone: 'A woman's reputation once lost is lost for ever.' This was the sum total of his formal parental guidance on the matter. But he himself was a model of somebody who had very puritanical rules about sex, in so far as women were concerned. Women who opened their legs before the marriage ceremony were damaged goods, in his eyes. Men were different, of course: sexually active men were just having a good time. What mattered was not the morality or otherwise of the act, but the perception of it. Reputation was all. 'Remember the eleventh commandment. Don't get found out,' he used to say in other contexts. Clearly it applied to sex, above all. If a woman's reputation once lost was lost forever, this suggested that you might as well be hung for a sheep as a lamb. You might as well go on sinning as much as you liked. For the loss of virginity outside marriage there was no forgiveness, no redemption, no second chance.

Alas, sex was the issue which finally killed what little trust remained between my father and me. The first Christmas that he and my mother spent apart, I had just left school. I wanted to go to a party in the West Country and was invited to stay with the parents of a boyfriend there. Jeremy was just what I had been wanting, those nights when I counted seven stars and made a wish. He was a dashing young naval officer and he was my first grown-up boyfriend. He had his own car, a smart sports car.

I did not tell my father I was going to stay with his parents, because I knew that he might not approve. We would have separate bedrooms and it never occurred to me or I suspect to Jeremy, that we might creep from one to the other. Instead, playing off one parent against the other, I had got permission from my mother for what I was going to do. But I should have told my father too. I let him believe that I was staying on his Exmoor farm. (At this point he had two farms, one in Gloucestershire and one on Exmoor.)

He was celebrating Christmas on the Gloucestershire farm. My brother and I were to spend Christmas Eve with him, then Christmas day with my mother.

He found out that I had stayed with Jeremy's parents. One reason for his anger was that these parents kept a hotel. This meant that I was staying with a family whom he considered his social inferiors. It mattered to him a great deal. Jeremy's grandfather was a rich grocer, who had made his fortune. My own paternal grandfather was a rich entrepreneur who had made his, probably with a great deal more sharp practice than the grocer had indulged in. However, my father had reinvented himself as landed gentry and had his own social agenda for my love life. This involved me marrying a non-titled, non-Catholic white Anglo-Saxon man with land! 'Never marry a peer, a papist or a pauper,' he warned darkly. Jews, black men, or foreigners were even more out of the question. Jeremy was none of these but his family, unlike mine, hadn't yet translated their money into land. Had they done so, my father's reaction might have been different. Like all socially insecure people, he did not like being reminded where he had come from.

It wasn't just that I had stepped out of line socially. The unforgivable sins, in my father's eyes, were those that made him look foolish. And, unfortunately, I had done this. For some reason he had rung the housekeeper on the Exmoor farm, asked to speak to me and discovered that I had left to stay overnight with Jeremy's parents. Did he think I had lost my virginity? I think it unlikely. In those days no respectable adults, and Jeremy's parents were respectable people, would have allowed a seventeen-year-old girl to share their son's bedroom. No. My sin was that he had been made to look foolish in front of his own housekeeper.

I acknowledged I was at fault, but he gave me the worst scolding ever. I arrived on Christmas Eve to face invective which seemed to go on forever. It was non-stop verbal abuse. When he finished, he would start all over again. He told me over and over, 'You're a whore.'

I was seventeen. I was a virgin. I had kissed Jeremy and been fondled above the waist by him. In 1961, this was reasonably normal, if a little fast, for seventeen-year-olds. But then my father didn't ask what I had done. He just raged and raged at me. I thought he would never stop. It went on for about four hours. I was so frightened that for the next six months or so, I hated each weekend I had to stay with him. Although I was meant to have a choice about which parent I stayed with, I did not take the chance to avoid him. I spent weekdays with my mother and weekends with my father. I would happily have never seen my father again, but somehow didn't feel I could do this. I hope I felt some kindness towards him, as well as duty.

During each weekend he would make some snide remark about Jeremy, just to remind me of his anger. He often threatened to shoot Jeremy, a threat that I took seriously. I wrote to Jeremy and called off our relationship without telling him why. It seemed impossibly embarrassing to tell him about the threats, even to save his life. What if he tried to explain things to my father? He might even come to visit him and tell him that we had done nothing wrong. And then what if my father did shoot him? I seriously thought he might.

My fear was enormous. I remember sitting on a train on my way to visit him and reading about the concentration camps in a paperback book which had just been published. I compared my fate to theirs. I felt as if going by train to my father's house was like the Jews' journey towards a concentration camp. As I write this now, I am conscious that even to make the comparison is to belittle the horrors of the Holocaust. But I put my feeling down as a matter of record, because it gives an indication of just how frightened I had become of my father.

How did this affect my spiritual life, you might say? It gave me the feeling that the sexual issue was all or nothing, and I definitely didn't want nothing. It made me even more anxious to desert Christianity. If this was how sexual celibacy was enforced on women, I was of the devil's party and I was glad to be. If I was to be called a whore for some relatively innocent kisses, then I would be one if I chose to. I would step out of the sexual line altogether. I would ignore the old morality with its cruelties. I would rebel against the unjust, uncharitable rules of that generation. Christianity said you should not have sex before marriage or outside marriage, but these rules were a sham. They didn't apply to men. They were just there to trap women into unhappiness. I had become a sexual outcast in my heart well before I had done the deed which would forever make me a fallen woman in the eyes of my father.

In those days the double standard flourished, and not only in my father's mind. The world of 1962 was one where sexual rules were enforced through threats and punishments on women but not on men. When I arrived at Cambridge University, Newnham College used to expel for a whole term any woman found with a man in her bed. The man would usually be treated leniently by his male college. The men's usual punishment was a week's confinement to college during the evening. Any woman who got pregnant was expelled altogether by her female authorities, unless she married the father.

Punishment was the order of the day for young women undergraduates who were caught out in full sexual intercourse. Those whose lives were already ruined by illegitimate pregnancy would be further ruined by the abrupt withdrawal of their education. This would heap financial difficulties upon social shame, but as far as I could see this did not concern the College authorities. Unwanted pregnancy was the sign of bad morals, rather than a welfare issue. They had no idea whatsoever of helping their female students. We were assigned a 'moral tutor' who was apparently responsible for looking after our welfare. In my first year, I only met this woman when asking permission (as was then necessary) to go to London for the day. She made no attempt to get to know us as individuals and certainly did not seem the kind of woman I would have chosen to confide in. A much more sympathetic woman took her place in my second year, but she had, I thought, probably to obey the college rules. So although I discovered years later she was completely trustworthy, I did not wholly trust her. I trusted very few adults at this time. Adults were the enemy.

Consequently, pregnant women students (and luckily I never was one) usually tried to find illegal abortions. These were risky to both health and happiness. Some young women would experiment with hot baths, throwing themselves downstairs, or overdosing with quinine, which was in those days available over the counter. (I gave myself one of these overdoses, at a time when I thought I might be pregnant. It produced a temperature of about 104 and, thank goodness, my period.) Frantic young women would go through these self-harming acts, in the hope of dislodging a baby, rather than turning for help to the College authorities. They were there to discipline, not to help. These were the days when Christian organisations, while providing mother and baby homes, were also routinely unkind to unmarried mothers. (They, like so many others, only started being kind to unmarried pregnant women once abortion was legalised and that kindness was directed towards the unborn child, not the mother's welfare.)

No wonder unmarried students turned to abortionists for help, and luckily, some of those offering abortions were qualified doctors. But even a medical doctor would not dare to offer aftercare. I remember one girl who came back after the operation in the doctor's surgery. She ran up a high temperature that night. In a panic I rang the doctor for help at his home number. I received no help, merely an angry refusal to be involved and instructions never to contact him again.

This was the old world, which seemed to me part of the Christianity that I had left – a world grossly unfair to women, punitive to those in trouble, and heaping shame on the fallen. The woman was usually blamed if a couple transgressed, just as Eve had been blamed for Adam's fall. John Milton's account of how Eve tempted Adam, had helped persuade me that Christian theology was irredeemably biased against my sex. I remember asking one practising Catholic man about birth control. He was a handsome young man with an impressive seduction record and I was considering going to bed with him. 'Do you use French letters?' I asked. He explained that he didn't. Seducing a girl was simply a small sin of the flesh, according to his confessor, he told me. Using condoms was a big sin and his confessor wouldn't let him get away with it. I raged. It was another black mark to set in the ledger of my complaints against God. A cruel God to all humankind but a specially cruel one to women.

So I set off down the primrose path of dalliance, following what seemed the enlightened devices and desires of my own heart, determined to enjoy myself and to make proper and rational use of the new sexual freedom which was on its way. In those days before the contraceptive pill, I had with difficulty found the only form of female contraception, the cap. The gynaecologist who gave it to me strongly believed that sex before marriage would prevent very many unhappy marriages coming into being in the first place. It was in pursuit of this sexual freedom that I deliberately let slip away my first great love affair, which had lasted for two years. I gave up real love with sex, for sex without love, because going to bed with only one man seemed a mistake to me. How could I tell if we were sexually compatible unless I had a proper standard of comparison?

The ideology of freedom had its price which I paid without realising I was paying. After a visit to my gynaecologist who had rebuked me for not taking advantage of the cap by further sexual experimentation, I set off on my bicycle with my new equipment determined to go to bed with a second man just to see what sex was like. He whom I had chosen was, alas, out. But within a day or two I found what I wanted. And yes, it was exciting with another man. Such excitement that I hardly noticed that it wasn't love. Indeed in a way, the lack of love made it easier. Having sex was less troubling to me than making love. It meant less. It touched me less. I could stay apart from the person. I was invulnerable. There were no responsibilities, nothing that might trap me. Easy is the road that leads to the hell of self-harm.

I never told my real father that I was no longer a virgin. If he had called me a whore for a bit of snogging, this would presumably have led him to cut me out of his life altogether. I would have been for ever unforgiven. I simply concealed this sexual side of my life from him. It was the only way we could keep a relationship going. We reached a sort of truce, as I became more confident that he could never know for sure what I was up to, and he became happier in his life generally as he married for the second time. We retrieved some love between us. I still feared him, as much as I loved him, but I had found a way of staying in touch. It wasn't just the sexual side of my life which I concealed from him; I concealed my whole love life. Never again did I go out with a boy who came from a family he knew. I never took my boyfriends home to meet him. The only exception was my first great love whom I had hoped to marry, my first husband and then my second husband. I reckoned my father had to meet them once before the wedding. As long as I never told him the truth, and lied if asked about it, I could continue to be his daughter and he would not cast me out of the circle of his love.

God was a different matter. I didn't have the same incentive to keep in touch with God. I didn't love him and it seemed extremely unlikely that he loved me. Why should he? Fathers who disapproved of their daughters' behaviour cut them out of family life. I could only stay within the circle of my father's love by outright deceit. Clearly this wouldn't work with God and I didn't enjoy having to lie. Some people can believe in God and not let God bother them: I couldn't. Why should I want to stay within the churchgoing circle anyway? It was dull, boring, and consisted mainly of having to kow-tow to him with a series of ceremonies. I didn't want church ceremonies of any kind. I certainly wasn't going to go through the farce of a white wedding, prancing down the aisle knowing that I didn't believe a thing and that the white dress was a lie. Nor was I going to swear to honour and obey a husband. Nothing on earth would have induced me to make that particular vow to any man.

Besides, I trusted in my own energies and intellect. I was of the new liberated generation who were going to change the world. The old stuffy rules (and I mean mainly the sexual rules) were outmoded relics of the past. We Sixties young people were going to be different. I looked forward to that new dawn when women wouldn't have to get married just because they were pregnant, when women and men would truly be equal, when marriages that were a mistake could be cleanly put away without blame. Christianity was on the opposing side. It stood for the old way of doing things.

I didn't need God. Why should I? What could God do for me, except tie me up with the old rules and make me do all those boring ceremonial prayers. He was no help to me, just a kind of tyrant in the sky who made life difficult for humans, more of a hindrance really. And the stuff about Jesus was all made up. It wasn't true and it hadn't happened. It was all a con. The very word, ' God', made me angry.

The only good life was a life without God. I just wanted to be happy, joyful and free. God could get lost.

CHAPTER SEVEN

DON'T CARE,
CAN'T CARE

But it wasn't God who got lost. It was me.

My lack of direction and my general confusion became evident when I had left my first husband. It had been a marriage that was unhappy from the first month onwards. He had a bitter tongue, criticising me in front of others for my behaviour and my looks. He lived off my money yet failed to help in any way whatsoever with domestic chores. As a 'wife' he was a failure, as a husband he was even worse. 'I'm a miserable sod and you won't make me happy,' he said with honesty. With the arrogance of youth, I listened but did not hear what he said. I was sure that I could make him happy.

Not only did he stay resolutely unhappy, he turned out to have a taste for domestic violence. A slim, apparently passive man, he had nevertheless, I discovered after marriage, beaten up the girlfriend who preceded me. After about eighteen months together, it was my turn to get hit. During a row, he struck me on the face a couple of times, so I hit him back and tried to bite him. I was too naïve to realise that even a slim man can usually out-punch a woman. Traditional public school education in Britain in those days had included boxing. He had learned this, as well as various combat techniques in the British Army where he had done national service. I was losing the fight when he

109

pulled me to the ground and started banging my head against the floor. It occurred to me that he might unintentionally kill me. So I stopped fighting back, made my body go floppy and feigned unconsciousness. At this point he stopped banging my head against the floorboards, got up and went downstairs to pour himself another drink. I ran out of the house and lived to tell the tale.

I didn't call the police, because in those days they never interfered in what they called 'a domestic'. Besides, I felt ashamed of being a beaten-up wife. It was a time when men were allowed to beat up their wives and women were expected to put up with it. As a hot-shot barrister told me, when a year or so later I was consulting him about divorce, 'One episode of marital violence really isn't cause for a divorce. Now, if he had beaten you up three or four times, then we could get a divorce with it.'

After that fight, I felt every day that I was living with an enemy. At all times I was conscious that if he got angry he might do it again. So I went back to my old childhood way of coping, which was to keep out of his way as much as possible, tell him very little, stay quiet and try to keep the peace.

It also began to dawn on me that while I was around to pay the bills, he would never bother to earn sensible money. My marriage was turning out worse than my parents' one had been. My father had been a generous provider to his wife and children. He had never hit my mother. When he met my first husband, he'd said to a friend: 'She must be mad to marry him. Like father, like daughter.' But in truth, he had been saner than I. There was some excuse for his choice of unsuitable wife. They had not known each other long and their incompatibility was not entirely foreseeable. For me there was less excuse. All that enlightened consumer sex should have ended in a wiser marriage choice, a choice not distorted by sexual desire. So much for the youthful arrogance of thinking I could do better than the previous generation.

Why on earth had I married this man? I was young, attractive and successful at my job, and I chose to marry a drunken man whose first wife had sensibly left him. I had even paid for his divorce, surely a sign that he was not going to be the model of financial prudence. I didn't love him; I just felt sorry for him. Perhaps I thought he was all that I deserved. I had imagined, because he was a weak, rather camp individual, that he would be less frightening than my father. Perhaps, unconsciously, I saw my victim-mother in his behaviour and she, after all, had loved me. But I married a victim only to discover that the victim appearance concealed an abuser. I learned the hard way that weak men are cruel. Only strong men have the confidence to be gentle.

It was in the first few months after leaving my husband that I discovered the joys of truly liberated sex. Or rather, I discovered the compulsions and excitements of instant non-intimate sex. There had been earlier foreshadowings of this in my life before marriage, when I had taken the fashionable 1960s view that only by sampling sex with different men, could I make sure that I would have a sexually compatible marriage. I had therefore deliberately engaged in a bit of judicious sleeping-around. What a mockery that was. It wasn't judicious at all. It was the early slopes of a downhill ride which looked as if it might go out of control at any time. The ease with which I slept with several other men frightened me. There never seemed any reason not to.

So, fearing my own sexual wildness, I had decided to

marry. 'But if they cannot contain, let them marry: for it is better to marry than to burn,' said St Paul. Brought up as a child in a marriage which hurt and degraded both my father and my mother, I should have known better than to see marriage as a cure for lack of sexual control. As a way of stopping myself sleeping around, I had chosen a man who spent every evening in the pub and didn't even pretend to love me. I should add, in fairness to him, that he didn't particularly want to marry me either but I suppose the offer of my financial help appealed to him. I blame myself for the marriage: I manipulated him into it. I don't blame myself for the subsequent months of unhappiness culminating in his violence. When the marriage broke up, as it surely was bound to, I went back to my habit of sleeping with anybody who seemed in favour of the idea.

The worst episode was when I woke up in bed with a stranger. I had never seen him before in my life. I did not know his name. I could not remember where I had met him or anything about the evening before. As we were in bed without any clothes on, I had to assume that we had had sex. The words 'making love' do not apply in these circumstances.

Not that I cared much either way. I did not care that I could remember nothing of who he was, how or where I had met him, the moments leading up to sex, or, indeed, the sex itself. Understandably I did not care about this utter stranger. Less understandably, I did not care about myself, my happiness, my well-being or even my physical safety. Indeed, I cared less for myself than for this stranger in the bed.

'What's your name? I can't remember anything,' I said to him. My mind was a complete blank about the night before. He told me. Nearly thirty years have passed and I can only recall his first name, Adrian. Indeed, why should I have bothered to remember his surname? It slightly surprises me that I remember even his first name. He was of no importance in my life, except as a kind of marker for that moment of recklessness. 'Don't care was made to care,' ran the old nannies' saying. Wrong again. Nothing can make don't care, care for herself. Don't care is the sister of despair.

'I'm looking for somewhere to live,' said this man with whom I had had completely forgettable sex. Always anxious to please, I volunteered to go later that morning and investigate some new flats in the City of London, both on my own behalf and, separately of course, on his. Politely, I initiated sex again. I didn't want to particularly, but it seemed the polite thing to do in the circumstances. One-night-stand etiquette seemed to demand it. One had to pretend that the morning after had the same enthusiasm as the evening before. Otherwise, he might correctly deduce that I didn't want even to touch him, that the closeness of his body made me sick with horror. His feelings might be hurt. Mine? I didn't even think of mine. Besides, he would enjoy the use of my body, and why should it not be used? If nothing else, I could be useful to others.

A few years back my father had called me a whore, but at least prostitutes sleep with men for the money. There is a reason for what they do, even if what they do proceeds from self-hatred, as well as the desire for the fee. There are also people with strong and healthy sexual appetites who genuinely enjoy one-night-stands in a relaxed and happy way. I am not one of them. Yet one-night-stands is what I kept doing. I would try not to. I would shudder at the thought of yet another one. I would say to myself, when an evening began, that this time I would go home alone. I would fully intend to do this. And then I would go home with some man. I devoted time and energy in attempting to make sense of my behaviour, to no avail. Since I was going to do it, whether I wanted to or not, I had better enjoy it, or try to.

For a year sex became a sort of mental obsession. Why could I never think of a reason to refuse? There were sensible reasons for saying no, which had nothing to do with moral rules, but I couldn't feel their weight. It would seem sensible to refuse if I didn't like the man, if I didn't know him well enough, if I didn't find him attractive. But these reasons were not enough. If he wanted sex, why shouldn't I spread a little happiness? As for my own happiness, well, that didn't matter. I was there to be useful, to be used. I was a body for others, not for myself.

This being so, I had sex with people I didn't even desire. Sometimes my behaviour was caring – not to myself but to others. I remember going to bed with a young man who was very unhappy. I didn't much enjoy it, but I made myself repeat the experience a week or two later, just to make sure he would feel that I had enjoyed it even though I hadn't. I look back on those two sad nights and see that in a way I was showing loving kindness, putting somebody else's needs before my own, acting out of selflessness. In a tortured kind of way it was a morally good act. Or was the selflessness just another temptation to self-destruction?

There was even an occasion when I was beaten up by the drunk man in my bed. For no reason at all he started landing blows on me and I was too stunned to get out of bed. So I lay on my stomach, taking the blows on my back where it would hurt less. I felt, anyway, that I deserved them. The man who was beating me up was only doing to me what I felt I should do to myself. He was somebody I had known for several years but, naturally, I had not known that he was prone to beating people up after sex.

Those once-only sexual encounters had their good points – when I could remember anything about the experience. They were exciting and thrillingly risky, as well as occasionally physically satisfying. Yet I cannot have been seeking straightforward pleasure, because I knew that a better way to sexual pleasure was a longer-lasting relationship. Somehow at that period of my life what I wanted was something which filled up the inner loneliness and kept at a distance the dark failure of my marriage. Close to somebody else's warm body, it was possible not to feel alone. Also, although they were potentially physically dangerous, they were emotionally safe. I might get beaten up but there was no chance of emotional hurt. They did not know me well enough to wound deeply. Without intimacy sex seemed somehow less frightening – just a matter of bodies.

Why did I hate myself so much? I do not attribute it directly to the results of leaving the church. The world is full of atheists who have no difficulty in leading healthy and happy sex lives. The devices and desires of their hearts are relatively benign: my heart, my inner self, seems different. Left to my heart's own devices, without the help of people and loving structures, I behave in a way that hurts me. I cannot rely on myself, as others can. I could blame the sexual liberation ideology of the time for my unhappy sexual behaviour, but I do not think that would be truthful of me. True, the Sixties and Seventies slogans of 'Make love not war' made it easy for me to refuse to see what was happening.

The propaganda pretended that sex could never be used as a weapon. I used this simplistic ideology of always-harmless, always-fun sex to cover up the harm it did to me. So the ideology helped me in my self-deception. Psychiatrists call this kind of thinking denial. I denied that what I was doing hurt me emotionally and was dangerous physically. I labelled the behaviour 'fun'. That curious label helped me ignore the fact that some of it, even most of it, was not fun at all.

Perhaps in a Victorian age, I would have been protected against such sexual acting-out, but I, not the cultural attitude of my time, was responsible for hurting myself in this way, using sex as a weapon against myself. Sometimes in the hot embrace of a man I didn't much like, I would wish that sex could go on until I lost consciousness, until I no longer existed. I began to feel as if my body didn't belong to me, as if it was a sort of machine, in which I was a passenger rather than a driver. In my own eyes I was an object, not a person, once I entered the bedroom. It was like watching depersonalised pornography, only I was doing it too. Luckily for me there was no AIDS virus in those days, so it was a case of slow psychological self-harm rather than physical suicide. There was no God in my life that could rescue me, it seemed. I had refused to believe in God, and anyway the only God that I did believe in, lived dimly but horribly in the back of my mind and would simply have condemned me all the more. He was like the quiescent volcano, rumbling threats most of the time if you listened hard enough, which I tried not to. Not dead, not living either, but still there as a malign presence. I feared him greatly. An eruption of God into my life would have been a horrifying experience. He would only have made things worse by adding the threat of afterlife hell to the hell that I was already living in. In the medieval pictures of the Last Judgement, adulteresses and lechers are often shown naked, driven by demons. I was driven by demons that year of my life, let alone the next life. It wasn't the primrose path of dalliance; it wasn't even the easy road to hell; it was the helter-skelter slide downwards with hurt and bruises all the way and no method of stopping.

How odd it is that religious people, and religious writing, often seem to claim that each sin is the result of a conscious decision. The spiritual life is portrayed as a series of rational or at least deliberate choices. I suppose some bad acts are deliberate, but most of my then sins (for what I was doing was, if nothing else, failing to love myself as my neighbour) were repeated out of a compulsion aided by a denying mind. I could not see what I was doing to myself. Even if I had been able to see the harm I was inflicting on myself, I am not sure that it would have stopped me.

Those who have never been in the grip of a compulsion will find this behaviour difficult to understand. Yet a compulsion doesn't seem to yield to willpower. You may try to break the pattern occasionally, you may even succeed for a period of time, then suddenly, you are back doing it. Sex, drugs, alcohol, overeating, slimming, spending money or gambling are all human activities which some people enjoy and do sensibly. For others they become a behavioural disorder. Some of us nearly destroy ourselves with these activities. They can lead to suicides, accidental overdoses, road accidents, or illnesses like AIDS. In those days there was no idea that sex might become a behavioural disorder, even a kind of addiction. To moralists it was an immoral act: to their opponents a life-enhancing, harmless pleasure.

If God Is My Father, How Can He Love Me?

I used to thank God, the God that I didn't believe in, that I had turned my back on religion. Religion would have added to my pain. The pain of compulsive behaviour is not in the act itself, or even in the frightening but excited anticipation of the act, but in its aftermath. The morning after I would feel ill with guilt and shame. Why had I done it, again? The question was not one I could find an answer to, though various exotic hypotheses would float through my mind. Perhaps I just had a strong sex drive. The way to push away the guilt and shame was to overlay it with propaganda. Label it 'just a bit of fun' and the bad feelings would diminish. If the Christian God had been in my life, how much worse it would all have been. How terrible to be a Catholic and have to confess it each week to a confessor. At least life without God was safe from his reproaches, either the wrath and indignation of the old God up there or the sad eyes of a crucified Christ who, like my suffering mother, bore my unhappinesses in addition to his own. Either God the avenging tyrant or the guilt-manipulating victim was designed for my pain, not my happiness.

To stay safe, I had to build a wall of anger against God. I couldn't do that with my real father whom I loved. I didn't want to be cast out by him, so I merely kept my behaviour from him. During that year of excess and pain and shame, I simply did not see him very much. He would never know – he never did know – that his daughter was dragging home to bed all kinds of curious and unlovely partners. One good thing had come out of my marriage breakdown. I no longer judged my father so harshly. As a stern eighteen-year-old I had been convinced that I wouldn't make my parents' mistakes. By the age of twenty-seven, I had equalled them in being divorced, and had outdone them in sexual excess. The optimism of youth had dissipated. Nor did I have the same faith in my own efforts. My sense of failure over the marriage, even though there were many extenuating circumstances, was acute.

I couldn't lie to God in the same way that I lied, by omission, to my father. It was easier just to keep away from him altogether. So I did what other rebels against religion do. I remembered all the loving funny fellow sinners that I knew, whom religious people would condemn. Then I thought of all respectable virtuous people who were unkind and stuffy. When comparing sinners with saints, it is easy to prefer the sinners. And I am not the only person to favour sinners. After all, Jesus Christ did too. Life without God was lonely, so lonely that I needed company through the night. Pascal, looking up at the stars, said that the silence of those infinite spaces terrified him. A life without God, and without any spiritual meaning, had created these daunting spaces in the universe, but it was less threatening than life with God. It was rather like one-night-stands with strangers – frightening in some ways, but at least safe from emotional intimacy. I didn't want to be emotionally intimate with God.

Alcohol helped me bear my year of one-night-stands and sometimes wiped them out of my consciousness, which on the whole came as a relief. It was frightening to emerge from an alcoholic haze with somebody in the bed, look at them, and feel relieved that I knew them. On the other hand, when we'd moved into the bedroom the evening before, and I could remember every single action, I would have much preferred not to have done. Alcohol helped me through these times.

It was during that year of despair when I first left my husband that I began to rely on its help. But was it a help?

Alcohol sometimes initiated my misbehaviour in the first place. So although alcohol helped ease the problem, it played a part in its cause. Only I couldn't see that at the time. Indeed, I couldn't see the role of alcohol in my life at all. The morning after, I would wonder why I had gone to bed with some man I neither fancied nor knew well. Was there something attractive about him, after all? Was I just having fun? Was there something deeply psychologically wrong with me? Had my mother taken some kind of chemical during her pregnancy, so that I had been born with the wrong mindset? These were my thoughts. Not a single thought about alcohol.

Yet on every single one-night-stand, I had been drinking. The idea of sex with some unsuitable man took root in the pub, usually about ten o'clock, after about eight large Scotches. If I had been that keen on sex, why was I always drunk? The eager erotic enthusiast knows that the best sex happens after only a little alcohol. Too much means less sensation and sometimes complete failure. But I was blind to the way alcohol was twisting my life.

Love, and eventually a happy marriage with the man I am still married to, did rescue me from one-night-stands. It was a relief. My whole life changed for the better. I recognised in my husband a strong man who was gentle, a self-confident man who did not mind when I differed from him, a man who did not try to control me even when he thought I was doing the wrong thing. True love (and I am not talking about mere romantic passion) slowly enhances and ennobles everything it touches. If I am a better person nowadays, it began with my husband.

But even love and marriage couldn't put an end to the

excessive drinking. This continued and the pursuit of pleasurable drinking began to involve even more pain. Just one evening must stand for all the many evenings in which I drank too much. This was an evening which started in a posh London bar. Like many other evenings, I was determined not to drink too much, or rather not to drink so much that I behaved badly. So I decided just to drink a few beers rather than my normal large Scotches. I was there with old friends, and we talked and got drunk together. At about ten o'clock we separated. I was drunk, but not paralytic. I could have gone home. I should have gone home, but the determination not to drink too much had somehow vanished with those few beers. I decided to stop off for a Scotch or two in a pub further down Fleet Street, a street in the City of London which in those days was the centre for all major newspapers. As journalists came off their work shifts, they would move into the paper's favoured pub, so I could always find a friend or acquaintance there to have a drink with. This is what I did that evening. Or I imagine that this is what I did.

The next morning I woke up to discover that I was sleeping on bloodied sheets. Both elbows were covered with scrapes, raw bleeding patches, and bruises. Bits of grit and tarmac were ground into my flesh. I had no idea what had happened. The evening after leaving the posh bar was blank. I could not remember which pub I had been in. I had no recollection of how I had got home or in what circumstances I had acquired two wounded elbows.

Later a neighbour enlightened me about part of the evening. 'I found you crying on the pavement, Celia. So I let you into your flat and put you to bed.' I was too ashamed to ask her for more details, but I think I must have been lying on the pavement banging my elbows up and down, as I cried. I have no idea what I would have been crying about. At that time my life was going quite smoothly. My behaviour made no sense to me at all and I wondered why I had got so drunk.

In the intervals between working hard and getting drunk – and such intervals were rare – I could feel the pointlessness of my existence. Nothing was wrong in my life. I was happy with the man I loved, and reasonably fulfilled in my work. There seemed no reason at all for my excessive behaviour. I could not say to myself 'I drink because…'

'How do you live?' asked a woman friend one day. 'How do you make your life have some point to it?' It is perhaps significant that we were having lunch at a cafe which did not sell alcohol, so I can remember the conversation well. Her words shocked me. The question seemed to ricochet around my soul. I could not answer it simply by pouring a drink and making a joke of it. 'My life doesn't have any meaning,' I replied. 'I just grab what is going and then go on to the next thing.' I felt a sort of terror at my own answer. I heard what I said and my stomach rolled over at my answer. Was this how I lived? Was this really how I lived?

To make myself feel better, I decided that she was an odd woman. She had had a nervous breakdown, I reminded myself. That must have been why she asked such a strange question. Why on earth was it of any importance anyway? She must be an unhappy woman to need to talk about such a topic. I was a normal, utterly happy woman who just got on with her life.

Yet God can get through even to people who are

defiantly anxious not to get help. There were no visions, nor did a still small voice or even the booming tones of a Cecil B. de Mille, speak to me. No gigantic mystic hand stretched down to rescue me. It was much more ordinary than that. I had been writing for my then newspaper about the Salvation Army and had come into contact with a couple of the officers. They told me how officers have to sign a temperance pledge and I read their founder's book 'In Darkest England'. In it General Booth writes about the sufferings of the poor, sufferings often intensified by alcohol. In some way this implanted in my mind the idea that perhaps alcohol was not always a friend to human beings.

That same week my father-figure, Father Mo, the school chaplain, who had been dead for several years, spoke to me again. Not in the flesh but on a piece of paper. I was alone at home, getting drunk with a litre of wine. From a heap of paper fluttered a letter that he had written to me, when I was about sixteen. Why I had kept it, or how it came to hand that particular evening, I do not know. It must have been years since I had even thought of Father Mo. The words, in his familiar handwriting, were these: 'Live out your life as a happy child in the sunshine of God's love.' First I scorned them. Then I wept as I poured out another glass of wine. The way I was living out my life was neither happy nor sunlit.

Two days later I decided that I must do something about my drinking.

CHAPTER EIGHT

GIVE IT
A WHIRL

I began my new life with a terrible hangover and a sense of outrage. What outraged me was the discovery that some kind of God or Godlike principle had to be part of my new-found sober life. Turning away from drinking meant turning towards something different, something drastically different. Only by turning to God, or something like God, could I achieve safety from alcohol. This horrified me and made me very angry indeed.

For me, and I suspect many others, it was my own bad behaviour – sin, maladjustments, acting out, call it what you will – that put me in touch with God. Without it, I should have led my life in a state of untroubled and easy hedonism. But because my pleasure seeking was of the self-destructive kind, I had no choice but to find a spiritual aspect to my life. While others can happily lead a physical, emotional and intellectual life without any spiritual meaning, I needed, badly needed, something more. If man is the measure of all things, then my own life showed me by how much I had failed to measure up. I was terrified by the empty spaces inside myself, the inner equivalent of the silence of Pascal's infinite heavens.

It wasn't a fair choice when I chose God. It wasn't really even a completely free choice. Just as the helter-skelter of excess that preceded it had been a compulsion, not a series of choices, so the decision to look for God was a driven one and at the start a very grudging one. The only moments of free choice were those few seconds, as I sat with my aching head in my hands at my desk, in which I knew I had to do *something*.

My early turning away from God in my teens had been a deliberate decision to follow my own will, and my own will had turned into compulsive screwing-around followed by compulsive drinking. Yet in that turning away lay the first seeds of a future honest spirituality. Rebels may have many faults but they, at least, take seriously the causes they are revolting against. They are not indifferent. As a child I had at times loved and been attached to Christianity so strongly that a few years later I could be sure that I wanted no part in it. Love turned to hatred. My hatred of the word 'God' showed me how very seriously I took him. God was a positive danger to me. I had a sickening feeling that one day I would have to crawl back to Christianity.

And I did. It did feel like crawling and I loathed it. For when I decided that I had to recover from alcoholism, I found that the way most other problem drinkers had recovered was a spiritual one. It wasn't enough just to stop drinking alcohol. I had to make a new way of life for myself, seeking out new values. The mental and emotional landscape in which I was living was geared to drinking – a landscape filled with dark moments of self-disgust, an obsession with alcohol, impulsive and destructive behaviour disengaged from any moral sense, and a place in which the answer to unhappiness was more alcohol, which in turn meant more unhappiness. That had to go. Only by changing this pattern of behaviour could I be sure that I would not revert to drinking. I needed a God, or a belief in something greater than myself, as a barrier against the bottle. My life up till now – the way I thought, felt and acted – had been shaped by my drinking. Now I had to hand over my thoughts, my feelings and my actions, to the influence of something different, something better. Whether that Something had an independent existence, or was just a human construct, was completely irrelevant. Either way, I needed it.

The beginning of my new life was marked by no willingness on my part. On the contrary, I was reluctant to go anywhere near my old faith. Anger and defiance were the predominating emotions of the first few weeks in which I stopped drinking alcohol.

I would have refused to have any part in the process of recovery and conversion to a new life, but for my even greater fear of what more alcohol might do to me. It was no way to start a day by coming to, rather than waking up; by looking around the room to see if it was my own house, a hotel room, or a stranger's house; by walking out of a flat (*whose* was sometimes a mystery) to try to find out which part of London I was in; or, indeed, by waking from a drunken stupor on a train and getting off at the next station. One of my most frightening mental blanks had been discovering to my utter surprise that I was on a train to Cambridge, the town of my old University. By the age of thirty-four, I had not yet done myself serious physical damage. But the frequent large bruises all over my body and cuts on my elbows were the outward visible signs that my inner life was out of control. The serious damage was emotional. I could feel my own paranoia. I knew that I was not sane.

Those confident that they are continuously sane will not realise just how disquieting it feels when you know your inner sanity is trembling. The core of your being, which allows you to talk and act like a normal person, begins to blink like a defective TV screen. As I sat at my office desk, I was convinced that all my colleagues were talking about me behind my back, and simultaneously I knew that this conviction was mad. Here was another reason why I had to do something.

So I had to try and find a relationship with Something – a God, a force, a set of spiritual principles, a source of strength outside myself. You could mess about with the words, but fundamentally it meant giving up my old way of thinking and being willing to try a new and better one. In order to get well, and stay safe from the slow suicide of drinking, I needed to develop some sort of spiritual life. I needed to give my life a meaning that would protect me against myself.

My anger at this was immense. I had turned my back on Christianity and opted for the freer, more rational life, as it seemed. The old Christian life had been not so much a difficult path as a dull and ungenerous one. It had been ruled by a God who sent sinners to the endless torment of eternal fire, and was administered by a church riddled with tiresome silly rules. Every Sunday men put on suits and ties, and women put on hats. It seemed inexpressibly dreary. The Church I had left had been on the side of conventional English life – Sunday worship, no sex before marriage (and look what that had done to my parents!), no divorce (and look how my parents had suffered before they broke that rule!), the casting out of homosexuals, and odd little rules like not eating breakfast before holy communion. It held attractive village fetes, admittedly, but these were hardly enough to hold a teenager in its community!

At the beginning of my recovery from drinking, my fear and dismay grew. If alcoholism was an illness, as the name implied, it seemed to me contradictory and bizarre that the cure was a spiritual one. And in the course of the first few weeks I came across people who were spiritual bullies. They made it worse. 'It's not enough just to stop alcohol,' they would say. 'If you don't take up a spiritual programme you will drink again.' They would threaten: 'You must do it this way.' 'If you don't get the help of a Higher Power, you will fall back into active alcoholism.' These were unreasonable, hectoring voices threatening me with a return to my addiction, trying to persuade me that only their particular path was the correct one. They increased my defiance.

These spiritual bullies then told me that I shouldn't feel what I undoubtedly was feeling, which was virulent fury alternating with corrosive guilt. They said I shouldn't be angry with people. I should forgive everybody or pray for them until I did. They told me that anger was a bad emotion that would lead me back to drinking. And, of course, I got angrier with everything they said.

This tactless lecturing was well meant. I have behaved in the same way myself at times, when I have been arrogantly sure that I had the solution to somebody else's problem. Instead of listening and empathising with the pain they are suffering, I have tried forcibly to slap on my easy-stick solution to stop their suffering. This, of course, is tempting for the solution-giver. It has meant that I do not have to do the much more difficult thing, which is to listen, affirm and in some ways experience, another person's agony. By offering, indeed insisting on, my solution I can cut short their pain, saving myself its backwash.

But it is bullying, all the same. Besides, nobody wants a solution pushed on them, even if it is the right one. If you want to persuade somebody, hectoring and lecturing them is counter-productive. So the spiritual bullies impeded, rather than encouraged, my recovery and what was to be my path to God.

God's greatest helper in my search for a new life, and thus in my eventual spiritual faith, was a militant agnostic with the nickname of Big Alex. He was a Jewish businessman and a hypocrite of the nicest possible sort. He claimed no spiritual beliefs at all. He never talked of spiritual concepts and he loathed those who used them as a form of coercion or bullying. In turn, they hated him for his forceful agnosticism.

But he practised, rather than preached, brotherly love. He listened to people, let them go their own way, and helped when he could. Indeed, much of his life was spent helping others. I felt he was my protection against the bullies. He freed me to be myself, to be human, by giving me his unstinting support in finding a new way of life. He also gave me some of the fathering I still needed, and perhaps shall need for the rest of my earthly life.

One of the great virtues of Alex was that he wasn't frightened or upset by other people's anger. He rather enjoyed it. So he didn't try to shut up angry people or cut short their wrath. When I was cross, I could let it out with him. I could be unfair, abusive and bitter about the spiritual bullies, egged on by his pleasure in hearing me condemn them. That released the anger out of my system. He never told me that I should forgive them or pray for them. He never told me that I shouldn't be angry in the first place. He just listened to and accepted my anger and helped me accept it too. And once the anger was out, I could forgive them. Indeed, once I knew that I could express my anger I immediately became less likely to be angry. Only a buried resentment is a resentment buried alive. Dig it up and it dies. Had I truly understood this mechanism for dealing with my own anger, it would have saved me the immense pain that was to affect me about ten years later. But I didn't analyse what was happening. I simply clung to Alex and felt safe with him.

Another helper was Danny Breslin, a retired railway worker from Fort Lauderdale, Florida. Danny was no intellectual. If life had been a problem to be solved, Danny would not have got to first base with it. He could not even do joined-up writing. He once wrote me a letter which was all capital letters, each separately and laboriously penned. His letters, like his speech, were unformed streams of consciousness. Many people found him deeply irritating. He often said the same rambling things over and over again. Danny hadn't learned to edit himself. He was an odd little man only about five feet tall, untidy, dressed in American jeans, trainers, T-shirt and anorak. He used to come to London every summer for about four months, staying in cheap bed and breakfast places. Every lunch-time he took sandwiches and ate them in the park or wherever he happened to be. He shared them with whoever happened to be around. You would see Danny sitting on a bench with a vagrant, both munching together. I am quite sure that Danny was not lecturing the man, though he might have been boring him with a long-winded and not very clear story. Like a parable, really, only longer, and less acute.

One of Danny's stories was about two men sitting on a bench in London's Hyde Park. 'They wanted to go shopping in Oxford Street,' said Danny. 'So one of the guys, he gets up and starts walking towards Paddington Station. After a while he says to himself, 'Jeeze, I'm not going in the right direction.' So he stops a passer-by and asks him, 'Can you tell me the correct way to Oxford Street, sir?' So the guy tells him, and he turns right round and starts walking back. After a while he's there in Oxford Street. He'd made a mistake, sure. But his mistake was part of getting to where he wants to be. But the other guy is still there sitting on the bench, going nowhere.' His conclusion, the punch line, was: 'So if it feels right, give it a whirl.'

Danny took care of me. At first I wasn't sure if I liked him or understood him, but I didn't want to be unkind by rejecting his advances. He took me for cups of tea that I later realised he could barely afford to buy. He told me his folksy anecdotes. He was another holy fool at the time when I needed one. His long, rather boring stories had simple messages. Just try and see what happens. Mistakes don't matter; on the contrary, mistakes are signs that you are on the way to where you want to be. When things hurt, it is a sign they are healing. Don't give people solutions. Just say and do kind things for them. Let them be. When you have something difficult to do, think of the easiest, smallest thing you can do, and start doing it – the secret of the irreducible minimum.

Danny's irreducible minimum was one of his best and I use it still when I am in difficulty. 'When you've got something to do, and you don't want to do it, don't think of it all. Don't think of the hardest part of it. Instead, just ask yourself this simple question: What is the least I can do towards this task? What is the irreducible minimum? Say you've got this letter to write. Don't think about what you're going to write in it. Just ask yourself what's the smallest thing you can do. That's easy. You can get a piece of paper. Then the next smallest thing is to get a pen. So you sit there with your pen and paper and you think about the next "least" thing, and you write down "Dear So and so…" Before you know where you are you're writing the letter. That's the irreducible minimum at work.'

Danny and Big Alex are dead, but there were other friends who helped me then, who are still with me. When I think of the acute pain of having to throw away my old life, come to terms with the damage it did to me, and start a new one, I realise that the only way I managed to do this was through the kindness of others. Kindness, rather than forcible direction, was what I required. I needed a good listening to rather than a good talking to. Blunt, tactless and forthright people were not much help. I shrank from them, and still do. People who said things like 'Take the cotton wool out of your ears and put it in your mouth' made me feel angry and unhappy. Big Alex, on the other hand, simply said: 'Most people talk a lot of nonsense, but it makes them feel better to say it. And when they are talking about their own experience, rather than telling you what to do, well at least that's true for them. So listen to that bit and pick out of it anything which might be useful for you.

Think of it like self-service. You take what you like and you leave the rest.'

Stripped down to basics, all the people who were trying to help me recover from alcoholism were suggesting the same thing – a new life, new thinking as well as new acting. And that did mean I would have to change my beliefs. 'I just grab what is going and then go on to the next thing' is what I had lived by as I swallowed one double Scotch after another. When I could not control the helter-skelter destruction in my life, I had become an active participant in that self-harm in order to conceal my lack of control. Besides, I loathed myself. I needed to have better rules to live by, for my own future health and safety. Love your neighbour as yourself and love the Good (or the God) seemed to be the commonly accepted recipe for a life without alcohol.

So I started the first steps back to my early ideals. The initial stride was the most important. I made a decision to search for the way. This was not necessarily going to be a route back to Christianity which still, then, made me shudder. Like the seventeenth-century dissenters (though far less in courage and persistence) I would become a Seeker. I would be a pilgrim, not knowing where I was going, but pursuing the unknown goal. I would look for the way, even if the way that was possible for me could not be the ideal way. In those early weeks I had grandiose schemes of reading my way through the world's religious literature, starting with Plato's 'Republic' which I had read many years earlier at school. Of course, it stayed unread, though I was to read a little of the seventeenth-century Christian Platonists.

If God Is My Father, How Can He Love Me?

What almost stopped me in my search before it began was fear of where it might lead me. If I started looking for God, where would it all end? I might have to leave my husband and become a missionary in Africa. I might have to give up the world completely and become a contemplative nun. I laugh at the idea now, but at the time it seemed a real possibility. And it frightened me. I couldn't see that a future life in a convent was unlikely, not least because I had never been nor intended to be a Catholic, not even a high church Anglican. Indeed at the time of my worst fears, I was not even a Christian. These anxieties showed that I was still seeing Christianity as something which would coerce me away from my true self; a religion of deprivation, self-denial, and victim-love. I was also thinking in an all-or-nothing mode – either militant atheism, or extreme Christianity. In my more down-to-earth moments I realised that no sane convent would have let me anywhere near the inside anyway! My sexual history would have splendidly protected me against that!

Another step took me forward. I decided that I would never worship a God who was morally inferior to myself, no matter what this cost me. This meant that I would judge God on my own terms and perhaps create a new God for myself. It has, for instance, always been clear to me that I, myself, would never condemn any living creature to an eternity of torture. Perhaps some human beings do not deserve to live. In the case of the irredeemable (if such exist, and I am not sure that they do), perhaps it is necessary or even merciful for them to be, as it were, put down spiritually. But I could not worship a God that refused to save the souls of Hitler or Stalin. And I certainly could not envisage a God who would condemn even these two souls to an eternity of pain. After all, both these men had once been small boys, beaten and abused by parental figures. As babies, they had not started life particularly evil.

The trouble was that this God of eternal pain was still alive in me, separating me from a new beginning. If there was such a God, then I would refuse to follow him. Better to be outside heaven altogether than to be inside, praising and glorifying that most terrible Tyrant. I promised myself that I would not require any attachment to that great Despot in the sky. I had the right not to believe in that God.

George Macdonald wrote some words which help stiffen my resolve when I weaken in my determination to stay away from God. 'Neither let thy cowardly conscience receive any words as light because another call it light, while it looks to thee dark. Say either the thing is not what it seems, or God never said or did it. But of all evils to misinterpret what God does, and then say the thing, as interpreted, must be right because God does it, is of the devil. Do not try to believe anything that affects thee as darkness. Even if thou mistake and refuse something true thereby, thou wilt do less wrong to Christ by such a refusal than thou wouldst by accepting as His what thou canst see only as darkness...' With the decision to reject that evil God I had cleared the first big hurdle between me and the way. If I was going to believe in a God, either it would be a God without any eternal afterlife whatsoever, a sort of Life Spirit or Spirit for Good, or it would be a God with salvation for all creatures.

It is one of the main paradoxes of my spiritual search, that I had to start with a refusal. To be true to myself I had to reject God, before I could find God. It took confidence to do this, and later my confidence and belief in myself was to falter, with a devastating effect on my emotional and spiritual life.

The Life Spirit, or the Spirit for Good, an impersonal force, was my starter God. As a God, the great Spirit has much to offer – sufficiently vague not to be cluttered with theology, impersonal enough not to be a frightening parental figure, remote enough not to be doling out little parcels of punishment or reward like a schoolteacher. It was a good start and I will go back to it if I need to. This Spirit for Good held me safe for a time in the way I was going.

After about a year without drinking, I could look back and find a new force working in my life, a power greater than myself. I hadn't felt it much at the time, but it had been there, otherwise how could I have done what I did? My own experience was proof that, with the help of Something, I was doing better than simply relying on my own efforts. I saw that I had been renewed, given new strength, redeemed. To put it in another way, I had been saved – from alcoholism if nothing else. Maybe this thing called God was to be experienced, rather than thought out. 'Comfort yourself, you would not seek me if you had not found me,' says Pascal. I considered joining an exotic religion to get away from Christianity. Somebody told me that in Hinduism it is not necessary to believe in any personal god, though it is also possible to believe in many gods. One attraction of this would be that some were female. All Christian gods were male.

Alternatively, you need have no Hindu god at all. 'Some Hindus put up a post of wood and worship it. What is important is not the post, but the attitude of the worshippers,' said a friend, how accurately I still do not know. This gave me the germ of another idea. The theology of the God I attached myself to might be less important than the attachment itself. My need for an inner vision might be more important than any exterior evidence of such a vision.

Trivial reasons also put me off both Hinduism and Buddhism. The Hindus and Buddhists whom I knew seemed to have to wear odd robes and learn foreign languages. I didn't want to do either. I didn't reckon I could guard myself from ridiculous extremes or absurd beliefs in a different religious culture. I had no way of judging what was 'normal' Buddhism and what was a cranky sect. I wouldn't know if my Hindu ashram was a ridiculous con trick or the genuine article. I just wouldn't have the feel for it because it was so outside my own culture. I couldn't be safe inside it. I didn't want to take the risk of becoming part of a cult.

I could have gone on my own way, with a spiritual life unconnected with any church or creed. There are many people who do this without difficulty. But I didn't rate my chances. The last time I had relied on my own enlightenment and my own efforts, I had seriously hurt myself. What hope was there that I could struggle into a new spiritual way without outside help? It seemed safer to feel the bulwark of an institution or a recognised religious body around me. I wanted all the protection that I could get in my new life. I was very worried that I would slip back into the old drinking life.

I also decided to steer clear of what I thought was intrusive religion. I didn't want to be pushed into something I was not ready for. I didn't want to be interrogated about my soul, or made the subject of public concern. I already hurt inside, with the pain of my past drinking. I couldn't face any kind of religion which made this inner anguish worse.

It was a deliberate decision, perhaps even a cynical one, to go back to Christianity. I had an instinct for some of it already, though I didn't believe much of it. But that didn't matter. I could take what I wanted out of Christianity and leave the rest, I told myself.

Did my new belief mean forsaking reason and rational thought? Perhaps so. The spiritual life I wanted wasn't one where all that mattered was having the 'right' theology in my head. I didn't have to give intellectual assent to the thirty-nine articles in the prayer book. If I didn't believe, I could attach myself, so to speak, to a noble lie. Better to cling to the nobly untrue, than to be left only believing in the efforts of a self which was likely to destroy me. A universe peopled with ridiculous but benevolent angels ('Turn but a stone, and start a wing,') might be better than those immense and solitary spaces in which I was lost. Perhaps I did not have the strength and self-discipline to live in that lonely, godless universe without hope. As a child it had terrified me. I used to stay awake at night, look out into the dark, think of all those millions of human beings dying each night, and feel sick in my stomach. The tiny size of humanity, the smallness of our planet compared with the galaxies of the night sky, made me too scared to sleep. So perhaps I needed the cosiness of a religion which would place those immense spaces into a moral, structured universe.

I couldn't properly assent to Christian theology, but

behaved as if I could. William James, the great American psychologist, calls this the 'As if' principle. He recommends it as a tool for a better life. For example, by acting 'as if,' courage can replace fear. If we 'feel brave, act as if we were brave, use all our will to that end … a courage-fit will very likely replace the fit of fear,' writes James. It worked for me in my search for God.

For several months I went church crawling. I tried Westminster Abbey, and the Baptist church a few blocks away, the Catholic church in my mother's village, my then local Somerset church, the Quakers in Somerset and the Quakers in the London meeting house just off Trafalgar Square. To these I owed a special debt. I might have become a Quaker, but for the fact that I cannot be a pacifist. I also seem to lack their inner calm. But a certain John Brown, of the Quaker meeting house, was leaving London and he gave me three books that he no longer wanted. From these I learned that Quakers won't be pinned down by theology and that they refuse to sign up to anything which defines the Christian faith. This refusal underlines the idea that God is not an intellectual concept to be mapped out. There is a kind of Zen quality about the Quaker faith. Its essence is behind or beside the words. You can feel it but you can't explain it or talk it out. Your own inner light is the way.

In the end the good old Church of England seemed the safest refuge. It is a church which does not make windows into a person's soul. If you turn up for a few Sundays, there will be weeks and weeks before anybody talks to you about religion, if ever. Indeed, I have known vicars who are extremely uncomfortable with any talk about God whatsoever, being most at ease discussing the prospect of fine weather during the next church fete. There are times when this apparent lack of interest in God among Church of England clergy, and their embarrassment in talking about such matters, is extremely irritating. But this kind of coolness and balm was what I wanted at the time. I wanted to be able to sit in the pew on Sundays and not talk to anybody about what I believed.

Besides, I found the familiar ritual from my childhood comforting. My own language, particularly the language of the Church of England's 1662 prayer book, is important to me. Words matter. I could find a little thread of faith in the rhythms of Cranmer's prose, in the same way that I could find a little echo of faith in the cool damp medieval churches of the British countryside. I clung to the culture and the ritual, though not the substance or theology, of my childhood religion.

I began to see that holding the correct theological map in the mind was totally unimportant, at least for me. There are plenty of people who believe all that stuff, and yet they don't even try to live it. Equally, there are plenty of people who sneer at all that theology and do live it. Big Alex would never have piously intoned, 'Love your neighbour as yourself,' yet he devoted much of his life to helping others. He showed me that spiritual practice is what matters. Spiritual theory can look after itself.

If the correct theological beliefs had been essential, I would never have been able to become a Christian.

CHAPTER NINE

A KIND OF
CIVIL CONFESSION

Seven months after I started my new life, I was working in the garden of our cottage in Somerset. The house was in a little hamlet of six homes, surrounded by fields and sunken lanes. At that time I spent my weekends and holidays there. Our cottage lay on the side of a steep wooded slope, called Windwhistle Hill. From our garden we could look up two grass fields towards a wood. In spring the wood became a carpet of green, then blue with bluebells. As the year progressed the tree canopy turned bright green then a dark green, and finally red and yellow. One autumn day I looked up to the hill. The wood was turning gold, scarlet and brown, as the leaves changed colours. I saw its glory. I understood that its beauty flowered because the leaves were dying. I accepted the transience of it. Wonder, understanding and acceptance of death flooded the moment, filling it with meaning. This commonplace wooded hillside, in the West Country, was imbued with the Divine. God lived in that corner of His creation and, through it, in me.

I accepted not only the fall of the leaves, but my own fall, my own decay and my own death. I foresaw my death without the fear I usually feel. I saw its 'rightness'. I saw how the glory of the moment depended on the transience of the leaf and of my own body. Death, truly, was a part of life. In the midst of life we are in death, and that death is what makes the beauty of the hour so full of wonder.

These words cannot capture that experience. I felt that heaven lay about me. Wordsworth said that poetry was emotion recollected in tranquillity and he could with his words recapture some of what he felt. I am no poet, and cannot recall the feeling, except as a pitifully faint shadow of its true self. I know it took place, but cannot re-experience or even re-imagine it fully. Nothing I have written here conveys the full wonder of that moment.

It was a spiritual experience. Its roots were in the dark years of compulsive sex and compulsive drinking. It flowered when I began to see the world in a different light. Once the alcohol left my bloodstream I could *feel* again. For the effort of giving up drugs, drink or behaviour disorders like gambling, overeating or overwork, often feels like a new life. Indeed, the decision to eschew an addictive substance or behaviour has to be accompanied by the faith that a new life will be possible and, eventually, enjoyable. We are born again, if only in a limited sense. I know that in the first few months of that year I saw the beauty of the world in a way that I had never seen it before – its shapes, colours, lights. This for me had a touch of God.

I also heard beauty for the first time. I had been deaf to music most of my life. I have been unable to enjoy the piano since I spent many years compulsorily learning it with a teacher who disliked me. I could not sight-read and my fingers would not obey the commands of my mind. As a result, I still hate piano music and turn off the car radio if the piano is being played. Some stirring of musical interest came to me at the age of twenty-one, but was lost as alcohol slowly took over my life and invaded my mind.

In the first months of my new sober life I rediscovered music – Handel's 'Messiah', Bach's 'St Matthew Passion' and Haydn's 'The Creation'. Is there anything more wonderful in music than the moment when 'The Creation' crashes into 'And God created great whales...'? Or from the 'Messiah', 'Behold, I tell you a mystery: We shall not all sleep, but we shall all be changed, in a moment, in the twinkling of an eye, at the last trump...'. When I hear these words in the musical phrases of Handel, it is perhaps the only time I fully believe them. At the beginning of my life without alcohol those musical phrases were more beautiful than they have ever been since. I cannot wholly recapture what they meant then. Haydn's great whales still crash into my ears, but without the splendour of that summer of 1978. Then I played the music over and over again. Then it was a spiritual experience, not just a recreational one. At times I could feel the notes spreading through my veins with a kind of rush of joy. Now I love the music but it no longer pours into me with the same intensity.

There was a spiritual spontaneity in all my reactions during that first year. I felt my way through the new life in a very simple fashion. It may have been a time of self-monitoring and of learning how I reacted to life, but the shades of the prison house had yet to close upon me. The rules and regulations that I was to shackle on to myself were not yet in place.

It was a time of wonder, but also a time of pain. Sex, drugs, alcohol, gambling and other activities done to excess, blot out emotional distress and sometimes even bodily pain. They blot out reality too. When you wake up after an evening's drinking, and the memory returns, you begin to feel shame, guilt and anxiety. But there is a remedy close at hand. Another drink takes it all away again.

So living a life without alcohol was like being stripped raw. There was no escape into oblivion. No friendly large whisky to make me feel better, to sedate anxiety, to cheer the spirits, and to take away the bad feelings. Even my body felt more pain. When drinking I would often discover huge bruises, the cause of which I did not know, and had not felt at the time. Now, without alcohol, I had the ordinary bodily pains of life – aching limbs after activity, and period pains. I was surprised to feel them at all. I had not been aware of them for about a decade.

Great surges of anxiety would sweep over me, as I contemplated going to parties or meeting new people without the support of alcohol. There were times when my self-conscious shyness reached adolescent levels. I simply did not know how to behave, while all round me others sipped their drinks and made the witty and amusing conversation which eluded me. Worse still were the feelings of shame and guilt, from which I could no longer escape. The burden of them was intolerable. Cranmer's words from the general confession in the Communion service expressed it in a way that the bland words in modern services do not. The memory of my drunken actions, my drunken speech, my unkindness to others, and my insensitivity, was almost paralysing. Other misdeeds, some even from childhood, came back into my mind, tormenting me.

And yet, at the same time, I rejected the idea that these misdeeds were sins. The shame, the utter blush-making hot shame of them, felt like sin. But looked at, intellectually, I hadn't done so very much. No murders. No great frauds. No deliberate cruelty. Just lots of drunken misbehaviour, some of which had hurt others, almost all of which had hurt myself. My intellect told me these were disordered acts, of varying degrees of seriousness, and that I had been ill, not bad. My gut heaved with guilt and told me that I was disgusting.

Going back to the helter-skelter life of a drunk would have been one way of making these feelings go away. Many people take that route. The other way was to get rid of the burden by talking it over with somebody. Confession is good for the soul, they say. It is certainly essential for diminishing that heaving knot of shame and guilt. As well as priests and ministers, we now have civil or secular confessors in the form of counsellors. I chose neither. At this point, I did not trust priests and ministers enough. Harsh religious words would have destroyed me. The church vocabulary, with words like 'sin', 'repent', or 'forgiveness', made me defiant. Little in my scripture education had suggested that confession was part of healing and renewal. I did not see it as a way to let go. It seemed more like breast-beating and self-flagellation, just one of the many unpleasant demands of religion – a painful process necessary to be good. You had to do it to stay in with God. Otherwise He remained angry or turned his face away. It was discipline or even punishment for doing wrong, rather than a way to salve past wounds. I did not know then that the word 'repent' can also be translated simply as 'turn'.

The turning away process involves severing the links to sin – not just in terms of future temptation but the links of past shame and guilt. The unspoken misdeed is more likely to be repeated, because it keeps its place unchallenged in the heart. Even if it is not acted upon, even if there is not the slightest impulse or temptation to repeat it, the sensations of shame remain. Without alcohol, it was extremely unlikely that I would ever fall drunk on the pavement, for instance. But the episode would have lived on in my head, thrust away from consciousness perhaps, but still there, able to shame me if it were brought to mind. If it was spoken about it would lose some of its power to hurt me. To be free of it, to be free of the shaming memory, I had to bring it out into the light, speak about it, and then, only then, would I be able to let it go.

I did not go to a priest or minister, but I considered seeing a counsellor. Alas, I did not know any counsellor I could trust. I worried that a therapist might make excuses for me or give me some complicated Freudian reason as to why I had done what I had done. I did not want to be told that some of my actions were only trivially wrong. I knew that already. If somebody told me I should not be ashamed of what I had done, this was going to be no help at all. I was ashamed, horribly full of a shame which could not be reasoned away. Nor did I want my shame to be reasoned away. I was clever enough to be able to explain my acts away, but nonetheless, the memories burned and burned. Explanations and excuses were not going to stop the pain of this self-torment. I wanted to be neither blamed, nor excused; I wanted acceptance.

In the end I talked it over with a friend who, like me, had given up alcohol. Confession to a reliable friend has a venerable history. The seventeenth-century Lord Chancellor, Francis Bacon, a corrupt lawyer but an inspired writer, acknowledged: 'A principal fruit of friendship is the ease and discharge of the fullness and swellings of the heart... No receipt (recipe) openeth the heart but a true friend, to whom you may impart griefs, joys, fears, hopes, suspicions, counsels, and whatsoever lieth upon the heart to oppress it, in a kind of civil shrift or confession.' Mine was not a general talk with a friend. It was particular – when, where, who, and exactly what had happened. A general talk would not have unburdened me. I told her my greatest shame and was comforted. I told her about everything that made me feel bad, including those moments where unease seemed to cling to perfectly innocent acts. I told her, for instance, how guilty I felt about coming from a relatively rich family. She suggested that when I feel guilt, I change the feeling to gratitude.

As well as talking to her, I talked to some of the people whom I had wronged in the past. Where I could do so without hurting them, I tried to make amends. This was another part of healing the past and trying to restore broken or wounded relationships. Sometimes this was difficult. I had said unpleasant things about a fellow writer to a third person. I decided I would not go direct to the writer and tell her what I had done. It might unnecessarily worry her and I knew that I myself would have preferred not to know about evil gossip. So I went to the third person and reminded him that I had done this, and told him how unjustified my remarks were and how at fault I had been. He did not know how to respond, treating me (I felt) as if I was a lunatic on the loose. If I had been looking for forgiveness, I did not find it: I only found embarrassment. Luckily, I was not looking for some kind of congratulatory pardon so, though the experience was upsetting, it did not matter. I had done my part in making amends for that past gossip. I felt better. The point of this process was to free me, as well as put right a wrong.

The intolerable burden slowly became tolerable. It did

not go away altogether, but it diminished. I am one of those for whom self-forgiveness is difficult and at times impossible. God may forgive me but I never will. Over the years I have had to confess and re-confess various moments in my life, as if only repeated confession can keep guilt at bay. For me it is not a once-and-for-all act, nor can the shame be lifted by an entirely private transaction between me and God. It goes too deep. Some of my life's actions, quite forgivable ones – like an early crush on a doctor, or failure to respond to an invitation because I did not open the letter – can stir up great gales of self-hatred in me. Indeed, at my worst moments I am disgusted with myself. The lifting of this burden requires a third party, a sympathetic human being, to listen to me. Only if I can forgive myself, can I let go of the past, and the presence of an accepting person makes self-forgiveness more likely.

After this secular confession, my relationship with my father improved. I began to see the good things that he had given me, and his many admirable qualities apart from his outstanding financial generosity to his children. Because of his lack of interest in me as a child, I was a prodigious worker. I tried harder than the average person. Thanks to the training in having to do things I hated, I had the ability to do what needed to be done, even if I disliked it. This particular quality helped me a great deal in staying away from alcohol. This was his gift to me. I remembered also how he had explained addiction to me, when I was about eight. Standing in the farm drive, where his favourite red hot poker plants were ablaze with flowers, he told me how he had given up cigarettes and explained that once you had become addicted to something, you must never touch it again. In implanting this idea, he unknowingly helped me, twenty-six years later, to recognise the way out of my difficulties with alcohol. I will be grateful to him for that conversation for the rest of my life.

I forgave him the unkind letters and any other hurt he had done me. Looked at from his point of view, I had been a disappointing child. But when I went through this process of self-cleansing, I considered only my own misdeeds and therefore saw only part of the picture. I wanted to take the blame that belonged to me rather than assign blame to others. This was the best of all possible motives, but it ignored some of the scar tissue which I carried through life. True, I was responsible for damaging myself with drink, but some of the emotional damage predated addiction. I told myself that I forgave all who had harmed me, and so I did. But true forgiveness is not just a warm and understanding impulse, it is a deep letting go. My unhappy childhood, though it may have been forgiven by me, was later to rise up and nearly kill me.

Fortunately, in the first months of stopping drinking, I discovered that I could use my alcoholic experiences to help others recover. This was a healing process too, as some of the blackest moments of my life became useful. After two or three years I could contemplate my drinking behaviour almost without guilt or fear. It was over, finished. I had dealt with it and now it was of use to somebody else. The burden of those particular episodes was lifted completely.

There was another requirement in my new life – that I should pray. It seemed quite impossible and very, very embarrassing. I still feel more shyness about kneeling in prayer, in front of onlookers, than I would about stripping. I have never knelt at the side of the bed in front of my husband, for instance. Somehow I just can't do it.

What is more, kneeling itself seems ridiculous to me. We don't kneel to anybody nowadays. In the sixteenth century, at the time of Cranmer, a son might kneel to his father to ask for a blessing without occasioning comment. In those days there was a culture of deference to all authority. Kneeling, curtseying and bowing were all part of normal social interactions, unlike today. I think they are now demeaning modes of behaviour. I would refuse to curtsey to a monarch.

Today almost the only people who kneel in public (other than in religious services) are those unfortunate people kneeling in preparation for their execution in troubled countries of the world. So for me, kneeling in front of God seems to pay knee service to a tyrant. I do not want to do it and I only do it in church, because it is part of a community action. And if there is a God who wants to see people kneeling, then it's not my God. It's the God I have turned my back on – the same God that seems to want to hear people speaking or singing praises. What kind of person (and God is meant to be a person) wants to hear a lot of lickspittle praise? These are all the trappings of the tyrant. Traditional Christianity still depicts heaven as if it is full of human beings kneeling and singing praises round a throne. We don't do that to our present-day monarchs, so the old image casts a very poor light indeed on God. Like so many religious images, it represents another barrier to a better relationship with God.

Prayer was also difficult because I felt I could not ask for anything for myself. I have known people who seriously prayed that they might find a parking meter and have told me that God meant them to be on time, so he provided one. I have myself occasionally slipped into this simplistic idea, thanking God for fixing my little moment of reality in the way I wanted it to be. But the implications of this thinking are appalling. Does God intervene, at the request of the faithful, to make little adjustments to reality? Should I blame God when all the parking meters are out of order? Should I hold him responsible when I ask for an end to a sick person's suffering and the suffering does not end? If I hold him responsible for this, then I must also blame him for the millions of dying children on the planet, the millions of suffering battery hens, the wild animals dragging wounded bodies till death puts an end to their pain, the starving mothers seeing their own children die at the breast. Is this the will of a God who stands back and lets it happen or, worse still, deliberately makes it happen? A God who is able to ignore the great chorus of pain-filled cries rising from the suffering creatures of our earth.

Worse still is the idea that pain is important as a kind of lesson to human beings from God. Back to the tyrant again, the God who tortures human beings just to see how they will take it, who puts them through agony as a kind of test. They will emerge stronger and better beings and win a crown in heaven. Those who don't, those whose pain makes them into 'worse' human beings (which I believe is far more likely), well, too bad. It's their fault for failing the test. Better a God who is not omnipotent than a God like this who is a thorough shit.

'I just can't do it,' I said to a woman who was recommending prayer. 'I can't pray for myself. It feels wrong, and I can't.' In retrospect, there was more than just theological difficulty in that feeling. I felt I was not entitled to ask for anything. 'Try praying for others,' she suggested. This, I felt, I could do. I used simply to hold them in my mind and send messages of love and support through the ether to them. These were my first deliberate prayers.

Then there was the problem of what language to use. If I didn't know much about the God to whom I was praying, what words were appropriate? The Spirit of Good, as my God then was, was a remote idea not a warm personality. The tug of the past helped once again. I found my old prayer book, sent to me at my confirmation by the vicar who had baptised me, my godfather, Father Goodchild. I read the old familiar words. In particular there was the prayer which asked for help in leading 'a godly, righteous and sober life'. The use of that word 'sober', so important in my new life, made me decide this was for me. I cut out the reference to Jesus Christ and began using it.

Luckily for me, I did not feel an intense antagonism to the Church as an institution, merely an antagonism towards God. The Church had not hurt me. I had not suffered from abusive clergy, cruelty in the name of Christ, or the mind-control of a cult. I have heard it said that if a church has abused us, we should go back and face the perpetrator. If we don't face it, if we just turn our backs on it, then we spend our whole life viewing that institution through the eyes of the child it damaged. The Church stays a monstrous and looming figure in our life.

In my case, the church and its clergy were not monsters. They had played a friendly role in my childhood. All I had to do was to give up the childish demand that an institution, in my case the Church of England, should be perfect. None are, churches included. We do not love people because they are perfect, so we can love an imperfect church if we let ourselves.

I began going to church, not because I believed in the creed, but because it gave me an hour a week in which I could pray and look at the spiritual side of my life. I have the greatest difficulty in setting aside time for prayer and meditation, so a Sunday service helps me do this. Even when my concentration is poor, the service seems to relieve some of life's stresses. When I started going to church, I promised myself that I would not require great feats of belief or participation of myself. If I chose to spend the time praying differently from the rest of the congregation, this was perfectly acceptable. By not asking too much of myself, I was able to join others in the pews.

I also read a couple of the Gospels right through from start to finish. In doing this I discovered not the Jesus meek and mild, but Jesus the young Jewish teacher, who was not a conformist, who was unmarried, perhaps gay in nature and unusually accepting of women and of foreigners (even the occupying soldiers of the Roman empire) and of heretics (like the woman of Samaria). And I have since realised that he experienced the full range of human emotions, including anger and despair: there was nothing goody-goody or pious about him.

It was a comfort to me then, as now, that he healed rather than shamed and blamed sinners. True, he told the woman taken in adultery to 'go and sin no more'. But his forgiveness was not conditional on her repentance – something that Christian thinkers tend to forget. We have no idea whether she regretted her actions and intended to reform and become a faithful wife. Jesus let her go, even if she was going to go back out there and straight into the nearest bed. Jesus also spoke about forgiving people again and again, in a way that suggests he knew very well that some people will re-offend. Once again, forgiveness is not dependent upon the offender's reformation.

Another great comfort to me was that Jesus saw little distinction between sin and sickness. When they brought the man sick of the palsy to him, he said: 'Son, thy sins are forgiven.' But the scribes felt that this was blasphemy. 'And straightway Jesus, perceiving in his spirit that they so reasoned within themselves, saith unto them, Why reason ye these things in your hearts? Whether is it easier to say to the sick of the palsy, *Thy* sins be forgiven thee; or to say, Arise, and take up thy bed, and walk?' He was not self-righteous. He allied himself with the outcast. He ate and drank and was criticised for it. He broke minor rules. He talked about the kingdom of heaven within us. He was not a victim, revelling in his own tragedy: it is clear that during those minutes in the Mount of Olives before his arrest, he wanted to escape the coming crucifixion if it were possible. 'And he kneeled down and prayed, saying, Father, if thou be willing, remove this cup from me: nevertheless not my will, but thine, be done.'

On the cross he suffered complete despair, including the belief that God had forsaken him. Those who say that despair is the ultimate sin – those cruel people so lacking in imagination – should remember that moment on the cross. We who feel rejected can know that he did too. He is a God who suffers with us. Yet there is a daunting recklessness about him. People talk glibly about following Christ. Taken literally, this must mean deserting family, giving up all riches, all treasures on earth like houses, nice clothes, furniture. It seems to mean never making proper plans for the future. It probably means giving up a sex life and all hope of having children. It definitely means embracing pain and shame and derision. There seems no room for happiness or fun in following Christ. We know that Jesus wept. There is no mention of him laughing. Apart from one wedding feast, there's little fun in what we know about the life of the young Jewish rabbi. Following Christ has also sometimes meant a martyr's death, like his.

People like me who have nice houses, lovely gardens, delicious meals, cosy families, and money in the bank are not literally following Christ. The minor inconvenience of giving some money away, but not nearly all of it, the difficulties of trying to be kind to others, the observance of prayer and involvement in community, cannot really be said to be imitating Christ. We don't even know if Jesus attended synagogue each Saturday. We know that he walked out of his carpentry business and became an itinerant preacher. He doesn't seem to have had money on deposit anywhere to finance his preaching. He certainly didn't have a nice house or garden, not even a donkey, the equivalent of today's modest car. He doesn't seem to have given away money because he seems to have had none in the first place.

I don't imitate Christ. I just daren't. And I can't see that I ever will. I've come to terms with this, but at the beginning my sense of failure loomed large and made me feel very anxious. On the one hand was the kindness and acceptance of Jesus Christ, offering me healing and happiness. On the other side was that extreme demand to sacrifice so much.

There was another difficulty. Although I had forgiven my

father and was making a new and better relationship with him, I had not really looked carefully back at my early life. Stirring up the past and analysing it was probably too risky a thing to do in the first couple of years after I stopped drinking. I thought it didn't matter, anyway. I was increasing my love for my family and my father, I was no longer drinking, and everything seemed to be all right. I did not realise that I would probably not bond with God properly if I had not healed the damage that had occurred to me in my human family. My spiritual life was becoming warped by the distortions of the past.

CHAPTER TEN

BEING GOOD, BEING NICE
AND BEING PERFECT

The first stages of coming back to God were like falling in love – the pain, pleasure and, above all, excitement of a new relationship. The human spiritual experience, though it is common to many, nonetheless feels completely new. It casts a fresh light on each day. Ordinary sights and commonplace actions are suddenly infused with a kind of glamour.

It is later in the relationship, when the first passion is over, that the difficulties begin. Or they did for me. Somehow I stopped thinking about the relationship between me and God and I started trying to Be Good. But for me this had very painful consequences. Traditional teaching suggests that Christians should try to be good. We have borrowed the Ten Commandments of Judaism and we should start following them. We don't, of course. We are told we should have only one God, but we have a threefold God which is contrary to Judaism and Islam and perplexing even to some believers, myself included. We are told we should not make graven images of that single God, but many of us do. Many churches have stained glass windows, carvings, and perhaps a painting or two. I have listened to sermons which have attempted to explain why these apparent deviations from the Commandments happen.

If God Is My Father, How Can He Love Me?

We must not swear. The prohibition against taking the name of God in vain, suggests that He is looking out for it. It's rather in the same way that those who believe in fairies refer to them as the 'people of peace' or the 'good folk', not because they *are* but because it is dangerous to offend them. The idea of a sacred name, almost a taboo name, is part of many primitive religions. There is, of course, a good secular reason for going easy on swearing. It offends others. But does God really keep count or care? Can a religious word, used as an expletive, really offend him? Is he that sensitive? That petty? If people swore 'Oh Celia, put that thing away', or 'By Celia, I'm furious', would I be angry or hurt? I suppose if I was a very touchy person, I might be. So, is God quick to anger?

The rest of the commandments are, indeed, useful guidelines for a well-behaved society. A day of rest seems a good idea. Indeed, secular society now has a working week which includes two days, rather than one day, of rest. The other positive commandment, which affects human relationships, is that we should honour our father and mother. Not love them, but honour them. This suggests that dutiful, rather than loving behaviour, would be acceptable. There's a certain flavour of cynical realism about it.

I have a memory of my own father dutifully visiting his mother. He would drive to see her every fortnight, a long drive lasting five hours. After a heavy, very British lunch of roast beef and Yorkshire pudding followed by blancmange or rice pudding with stewed fruit, he would sit opposite her in front of a tiny gas fire in the everyday sitting room, rather than the plush drawing room which was never used. A stream of gloomy platitudes flowed from her lips and slowly his head would begin to sink and his eyes would close. Then with a snort, he would wake up and straighten up. After a cup of tea, he left for the long drive home. My father certainly honoured his mother. I know he loved her, but he found her a terrible bore and so she was.

I began trying to honour my father and mother and this aspect of Being Good seemed to work quite well in my relationship with my father. When I didn't want to see him, I would fall back on duty and see him anyway. I still feared him. This fear only diminished when I became happily married myself, and then the visits became less anxious. But I might have broken off the relationship altogether, were it not for the fact that I was Being Good. Many of my father's other close family relationships had ended in rows and estrangement because of his habit of writing abusive letters or initiating bloodcurdling rows. He loved his family but could not handle disagreements and did not know how to forgive. But because I tried not to quarrel, because I tried to show love, a real if slightly remote friendship started developing between us. I did not trust him with any intimate revelations, and what was not said between us seemed a help rather than a hindrance. So my Christian effort to Be Good sometimes paid off.

My mother, who lived alone, received most of my care since my father had happily remarried. My attempts to Be Good to my mother seemed easier because our relationship was close. Here, a more subtle problem began creeping in. She was somebody who was lonely and emotionally distressed most of her life. She usually needed cheering up and I would try to do this for her. But now I began to start feeling her pain, as if it were my own. I remember one Valentine's Day, a Sunday, sitting in church and experiencing a great wave of her loneliness and unhappiness. I had sent her some Valentine flowers, but I had not gone to visit her and I felt guilty about not doing enough for her. I went home and rang her immediately. I had been feeling her pain by proxy, and only a long phone conversation could alleviate this.

'You need never feel guilty about me,' she said to me in the last year of her life, but I did feel guilty, almost all the time. A knot of pity and guilt is sometimes still with me when I think of her, although she has been dead for several years. I find it hard to remember her as somebody who was ever happy, though I am sure she must have had some happy moments.

Many of the commandments are negative and some were within my grasp. We must not commit adultery, steal other people's property, lie, kill, gossip, or be envious of others. These suggest that self-restraint must have a very high value. We are told what not to do, rather than what we should do. A person who kept these commandments literally would be an acceptable next-door neighbour but could nevertheless be a cold, unloving person.

Of course, Jesus Christ didn't put it this way. Borrowing from the Old Testament, he quoted: 'Thou shalt love the Lord thy God with all thy heart, and with all thy soul, and with all thy strength, and with all thy mind; and thy neighbour as thyself.'

Somebody with a light heart and a feel for the spiritual life will no doubt pick out what really matters from the commandments and that saying of Jesus Christ's. But if you have a heavy heart, as I had then and still have, they can be troubling in the extreme.

Looked at in a melancholy and literal fashion, it seems

that self-restraint and control of feelings is the right way to Be Good. With an iron self-restraint and a rigid control of feelings, you can avoid lying, swearing, and committing adultery. Count ten before you say and do anything. Smother all desires. Learn to deny yourself. Better still, murder feeling in its cradle and it will never grow up to commit vice. That way, if you kill feelings at birth, you will never feel envy. You will not feel pain either, or anger, or lust. If, however, you murder all feeling you will probably not feel joy. That is roughly how I set about Being Good. It fitted well with my early training. I had learned from childhood, from being brought up in the same house as my father, how to tread carefully. From a very early age I knew that I must not cry. '

So the best way to ensure that tears never fell was to smother sorrow at birth. As I successfully stopped feeling sadness, I did not cry. A kind of tight blank sensation, with dry eyes, was and still is my learned response to sorrow or distress. As an adult I normally cry only with pleasure. Anger also had to be rooted out. Anger was the privilege of my father. He was angry with my mother every day and angry most days with us children. Tears provoked his wrath, as I have said, but so did our own anger. If we children expressed anger, then he would respond more furiously than ever. We learned never to criticise him, always to be careful of what we said in front of him, what we did in front of him, what expression was on our face, what tone in our voice.

So Being Good by not feeling anger was relatively easy. I had reduced anger by the age of about eighteen months. 'You were a wonderful baby,' said my mother. 'You never bawled. You just lay silently in your cot with tears leaking out of your eyes.' I think I knew that to keep quiet was best. By the age of about eight I had learned to stop the tears too.

It was much the same situation with this God that I had returned to. I would Be Good by not doing bad things, and by smothering even the impulse to do bad things. If I controlled what I did, what I said and how I felt, I might be able to get it right. I tried to do this. I began walking on eggshells around my God. He became a God who wanted regular praise (or flattery), hated criticism, and also required regular dollops of breast-beating or repentance before administering forgiveness. If I could live with a frightening, authoritarian father, I could probably get by with a dictatorial God. Job, tormented by divine cruelty, submits to a God who says, 'Behold, the fear of the Lord, that *is* wisdom…'. I submitted and complied as part of my attempt to do the right thing.

I am driven by fear anyway. Most of all, I am driven by terror that I will get things wrong, make a mistake. And for me, even a tiny mistake is something shameful. Sometimes I feel sick with shame for several days, even weeks. Alcohol gave me the bravado to ignore these tendencies, but the sober life did not. Adding the rules of religion to a life already full of potential mistakes, increased the possibility of further errors. I knew that I could probably manage not to steal, not to murder and assuming my marriage remained loving, not to commit adultery. That all seemed relatively easy.

I seemed successfully to have murdered anger and sadness in myself, putting on a mantle of forced gratitude and cheerfulness. But envy was a different matter. It thrived in me. The more I tried to Be Good, the more it plagued me. Underneath my outwardly correct behaviour, dark envy flourished. It crept into my mind and I would try to push it away, but it would return in a different guise. I found myself reading and enjoying bitchy book reviews, unkind newspaper columnists and excoriating interviews. I would read these, feel envy, then self-disgust.

Being Good was also exhausting. It was a life of unremitting effort and self-consciousness. It's tiring and rather tiresome to have to monitor everything you say in case you use a rude word, or pass on amusing but unkind gossip. It produced in me rather the same state I had experienced in childhood, when sitting at the family table trying in vain to think of something to say which would stop a family row. This state of anxious self-monitoring is coupled with even more anxious monitoring of those around you. In my case, this Being Good meant living with a lie in the mouth.

My other guiding principle of Being Good was 'Don't hurt anybody.' This still appeals to me, as it must appeal to all those who have been wounded by the harsh words of others. I have never wanted to pass down to others, the pain inflicted within my family. Having had a father who repeatedly called me 'the runt of the litter' and 'the milksop', I have always hoped I should manage to get through life without telling others they are weaklings and cowards. I know the deep hurt that words can inflict.

But not hurting others only too quickly becomes Being Nice, the outer accompaniment to Being Good. Not only was I afraid of hurting others, I feared (and still fear) that others will hurt me. Being Nice is a way of protecting myself. My natural state is a desire to please. I will please the postman by smiling as he hands the letters in, the dustbin collectors by giving an unnecessarily generous Christmas box, the newsagent by talking to him about his children. At first sight, the desire to please looks harmless. But the flip side is that I am inordinately sensitive about not being liked. If a new postman doesn't smile back, I will feel a pang of disquiet which can last for several hours.

One of my weapons in the 'Being Nice' offensive was charm. 'Charm the bird down from off the tree. Don't throw a bloody great brick at it,' was one of my father's bits of advice for Life. Like him I have used, and still sometimes use, charm as a method of getting what I wanted. It is, I now realise, a manipulative and deceitful method.

I am also obsessed with conflict avoidance, and making things go smoothly is another of my besetting sins. Blessed are the peacemakers? Perhaps. But is there not in the compulsion to make peace, and avoid conflict, a fundamental dishonesty? I have felt anger in my heart and have walked away without showing it. It has burned the harder within me, but even stronger has been my fear of the other person's anger. I want to control events by being nice: if I am really nice, perhaps nobody will hurt me. There was a childhood saying which must have come from my mother: 'Is it true? Is it kind? Is it helpful? If not, do not say it.' So I spared others hard words, but I also often failed in the basic honesty of telling them how I felt. An encounter in which one person lies to another to ensure a peaceful outcome, is dishonest. Was this really a blessed peacemaking?

Being selfless was another phrase that somehow became entrenched in my mind. Making sacrifices was another. Doing things I didn't like was relatively easy for me. In my childhood I had done many things I didn't enjoy every day.

Each meal time had involved swallowing down some food I hated. I had ridden ponies for hours when I was terrified. I had been told I must never take the largest piece of cake or the best bun from the plate. I must not ask for things for myself.

One small example of the Being-Good blight involved our holiday home in Somerset. At that moment in my life I enjoyed being in London more than I enjoyed being in the country, but I would go to Somerset whenever my husband chose to, even if I didn't want to accompany him. I would stay silent about my own wishes. I would dutifully pack up the car and go down there with him. During the two and a half hour drive, I would feel hard-done-by. By refusing honestly to tell him that I wanted to stay in London and that he could go down by himself, I enjoyed a feeling of virtue mingled with powerful resentment. Sometimes I would be bad-tempered in the car and, if questioned, reveal that I didn't want to go. Then my husband would say: 'Why didn't you say so?'

I cannot have been much fun at these times. Martyrs are unattractive companions to live with, often using their suffering to manipulate others. I felt that I had been such a terrible wife during my drinking years, that I must now be a perfect one. 'We recovering alcoholics can never make it up to our husbands. After all, we caused them such pain,' a woman once told me. It entered my mind with the force of something that fitted the victim-martyr I was becoming. Yes, that was it. I had to be extra-good now. I must put up with things. I must not tell my husband if something he did upset me. I must pretend it was OK when it wasn't. I must obey my husband, like it says in the Bible. The perfect wife did what her husband wanted and never showed she was upset. That had clearly been what my father had wanted and did not get in his first marriage. But it is, of course, not what loving husbands usually want. Husbands love their wives, and wives love their husbands, because of what they are, not because of what they do. That truth escaped me. I felt that I must be self-denying and do what he wanted, in order to make up for my past bad behaviour. I tried to become a version of the Stepford Wives. Indeed, the habit of doing what others expected of me became so ingrained that I often did not know what I wanted to do for myself. I merely knew that I was doing something I didn't want to do.

Helping others was my other besetting 'virtue' at this time. This too came from within me, as much as it came from Christianity. I had been trained to look after my little brother from an early age and had indeed earned some praise from my father for doing so. With my brother in tow, I was an acceptable companion to him in a way I had never been on my own. And, of course, we children had tried to comfort and help our mother. In her life of constant unhappiness, we made strenuous efforts to make up for the unkindness inflicted on her by our father.

Show me a victim, preferably a helpless female one, and I will often spring to her aid without further thought. This started with helping other problem drinkers. I would try and help not just those who wished to stop drinking but those who merely enjoyed the attention of somebody trying to help. I collected emotionally needy people. They would ring me at all times of the day, spend hours on the phone, and still I would say 'Ring me any time.' If they phoned when I was eating a meal or going to go to bed early, I wanted to say, 'Please, I cannot talk to you now.' But instead I would say, 'Of course, it is all right, if you want to talk now.' I usually acceded to their requests.

I became the helper of the deliberately helpless. I lent money to anybody who asked for it. I gave away money unwisely. I gave money to an Australian who said he needed it to rescue a girl who was taking drugs in the Canary Islands. 'Shouldn't you just let her get into trouble?' I said tentatively to him. By then I knew that addicts only stop using drugs when they (not others) want to. 'I quite understand if you feel you don't want to lend the money,' he said. 'Why should you care if she dies from an overdose?' Horrified by the potential guilt of being responsible for her death, I gave him the money, knowing he would never repay it, and knowing, even as I wrote the cheque, that I was doing the wrong thing not just for me but also for her. He took the cheque and had a nice holiday in the Canaries, forcing his attention on a girl who was drugged out of her mind and who otherwise wouldn't have tolerated him. (She told me this later when she had stopped using drugs. Oddly enough, it was the horror of sleeping with the awful Australian which helped convince her that drug using was no fun!). My 'niceness' cost me several hundred pounds and, although I told myself that in a roundabout way it had achieved its objective, I knew deep down that I had paid up because I was afraid of refusing, rather than out of misplaced kindness.

Among my emotionally needy cases was the old lady round the corner in London, whom I visited at least twice a week. She was a compulsive talker with whom I spent hours. She was lonely. Nobody visited her. She was passive, sitting in her little flat complaining that nobody came to see her. It did not seem to occur to her that she might go to visit somebody herself. It did not occur to me either. I would sit there listening to the long involved sentences which would range backwards and forwards over fifty years of her life, an unhappy life with very little incident. In half an hour, she would talk for twenty-five minutes. She had forgotten, if she ever knew, the polite rules of give and take in conversation. And as she had no interest in others, even those present in the room, she spoke only of herself.

But who am I to pass judgment? Perhaps, like me sitting opposite her, she was blotting out her inner pain with these torrents of talk. I have been told that compulsive talking is an addiction, a way of evading an honest relationship with the self and others. We were both playing the same game, avoiding a proper human encounter, she by talking, I by listening. When I was being busy 'helping' others, I did not have to spend time with myself. Constant concern with others can erase inner pain very nicely thank you.

In all this do-gooding, there was compulsion rather than choice, and I did not see what I was doing. It was not just a series of generous decisions to help somebody. It was a life of being unable to say no. Years ago I had managed to stop having sex with men simply because they wanted it, even when I didn't. Now I failed to say No to different demands. I spent time that I could barely afford with lonely people who had plenty of time to fill. If I was tired, I did not rest. If I was unhappy, I did not cheer myself up by doing something nice for myself. If occasionally I gave myself a break, I felt guilty. I had to Be Good, Do Good. A new Biblical verse took over my mind – 'For unto whomsoever much is given, of him shall be much required: and to whom men have committed much, of him they will ask the more.' I had good health, riches and brains; I must justify these by toiling ceaselessly.

When I became short-tempered through tiredness, felt life was unfair, or if I began inwardly to complain, I would not listen to myself. Irritability and self-pity are, indeed, unedifying responses, but they are also a sign that inwardly something may need redress. Instead of asking myself why I was feeling this way and what I could do about it, I told myself that I was at fault. I smothered inner resentment with a kind of forced gratitude when a bit more rest or recreation might have been called for. I had so much in life, so very much, I told myself, that my sense of gratitude must never falter.

As well as compulsively helping others, I worked very hard at my job. Just as I could not turn down a request for help, I could not turn down work when it was offered to me. As a self-employed writer, I had an exploiting employer. The structure of my life was poor. I did not give myself enough rest. I did not set aside time for amusement or just pottering about. I skipped meals, unless I was cooking for my husband. I gave money to others rather than spending it on myself. I did not buy clothes. My underwear was grey and tattered with age. Sometimes my husband would have to buy clothes for me, simply because I did not feel I could spend the money on myself. I bought kitchen equipment from second-hand charity shops, even though I could have afforded to buy it new. Buying things for myself became increasingly difficult.

I did too much almost every single day. One concerned person told me I was becoming a workaholic, and I was pleased with the label. I was trying to earn my way in life. I was trying to justify my existence. I began chivvying myself into Christian orthodoxy and worrying when I couldn't believe all of its facets. I stopped taking what I liked or needed in Christianity, and began to feel I should swallow it whole instead of picking and mixing. Perhaps there had to be a last judgment; perhaps it was best if God was that fierce judge of all human beings, whose wrath and indignation against us was provoked by our sins. It is possible to force belief and I did. I even read the thirty-nine Articles at the back of the prayer book, among which are ideas fit to raise every hair of the head.

Once in the course of this ten-year period of trying to be perfect, I had got so depressed that I took myself off for one session with a counsellor. She knew I was a Christian and she said to me: 'You can't earn salvation, you know.' I think she was trying to tell me that salvation was a gift for the asking, not a reward for being good. But that is not the message I heard. I heard her say that I would not be able to earn salvation because I just wasn't being good enough. The words slid into my mind like a sluggish monster of the deep lying in wait for its prey.

Somehow, I had to pay back God for his kindness in helping me stop drinking. Clearly, I had got to try harder. I slipped into the habit of pleasing a God who was remarkably like my unpredictable father had once been – pleased only by obedience and unremitting effort. 'Be ye therefore perfect, even as your Father which is in heaven is perfect.' Christianity seemed to require this of me. After all, sacrifice was at its heart. The Father God would only forgive sins if the blood sacrifice was paid. Christ had died on the cross to fulfil this sacrifice and to pay for human sins. If I was to be like Him, I had to pick up my cross and begin mortifying myself. Every small discomfort inflicted upon myself would count as a Brownie point. Every time I did something I didn't enjoy, it would be a small step to becoming a better person.

A victim life, like the one I was beginning to lead, has its pay-off in the self-righteousness of the victim. It conceals simmering resentment or deep self-hatred, usually both, and neither is often apparent to the victim. In my own case, the anger at the way I was treating myself, was buried deep. Since I could not, must not, hurt others, the only person left to hurt was myself.

As well as turning away from happiness, I was haunted by a new sense of guilt. What I was doing was not enough. I should do more. I should give up my comfortable life. Was it not clear that I had no chance of being saved, since I was so rich? The correct thing to do was simply to give my money away, but I didn't dare do that. My sins of omission lay heavy on me and wouldn't go away.

Some structure of normal life remained because my husband prevented me from going too far in my actions. When I did something pleasurable, like going to a movie, it was because he wanted it. He kept some common sense in my life. I seemed to lead two lives. One was with him and our friends. The other was my secret life, as the do-gooder.

My inner self began to die a little. I stopped listening to the music that I had enjoyed. I did not seem to have time any more to do so. Simultaneously, the beauty of the world around me seemed to fade away. Some of this was no doubt the effect of eyes that were now accustomed to 'sober' seeing. But often I was so busy, rushing backwards and forwards, that I had no time to stand and stare. In one way

Being Good worked well. It stopped me feeling the unpleasant emotions of anger, sorrow or emotional distress. I had no time to notice whether I was happy or sad. If I felt angry, I knew that the feeling was a bad thing. So I would try to force it out of my mind or smother it deep down where I need not pay attention to it. If I was helping others, I wouldn't be angry. I became less and less able to feel anything. Joy diminished, but the big gain was that pain diminished too.

I had fallen out of love with God. What had replaced this was a desire to please entirely familiar from my childhood. Alas, there was plenty in traditional Christianity to encourage me in this way of living. If I was the child of God I had somehow got to earn his love. I must keep trying. I must not make mistakes. I must care for others rather than myself. Then perhaps God might relent towards me. Or he might not. After all, he had given me such great gifts already, that I might not have the right to expect more. I had a lot to live up to. And if there was going to be an after-life in which the score was evened up, then my future state looked grim.

CHAPTER ELEVEN

DAMNED
BELOW JUDAS

Hell gaped for me in 1989. I knew beyond all doubt that I was doomed to everlasting torment, cast out from the mercy of God, condemned for ever and unworthy of his love. Moment by moment I lived with this knowledge. The sorrows of hell enveloped me. Others have suffered this immense pain: we, who believe ourselves destined for hell, live already in hell in our own minds. Like another sufferer, the poet William Cowper, I was convinced that I was damned:

> Damned below Judas; more abhorred than he was,
> Who for a few pence sold his holy Master!..
> Man disavows and Deity disowns me.

I inhabited the darkness, cut off from all hope of light. Utterly outcast, I belonged to that world of wailing and gnashing of teeth, beyond the reach of God's grace. God had turned his face away from me.

This feeling was so overpowering that I could not argue my way out of it. The theological concepts of grace and redemption had no meaning for me. The idea of God's love in general terms was not difficult for me believe in. That he might love the world seemed to me quite probable: that he might love me, on the other hand, was impossible. It simply could not be. His love, freely available to others, was denied me. I was outside its range. I loathed myself. In my own eyes I was disgusting. It was not that life had lost its joys. I knew they existed for others. I could acknowledge, though not appreciate, the myriad beauties of the world around me, but when I turned my gaze on myself I wanted to vomit. I was the blot on the fair face of reality. I was contaminating the world with my presence. It would have been better for me and for the world if I had never been born. I recoiled from mirrors. Sometimes I shuddered as I looked at the being reflected there. It was so repulsive.

I remember one morning when I was dressing to get ready for work. I looked towards my husband and my heart told me that he would be happier without me. Poor man. Married to this revolting woman, this parody of a wife, this unutterably distasteful creature. If I truly loved him, I should relieve him of the burden of myself. If I truly loved him, perhaps I should kill myself. This would free him once and for all from my presence in his life.

As I write this several years later, I am conscious that my words do not convey the full intensity of those feelings. My self-hatred was utterly convincing to me. It was a given, a feeling so established, so very *there*, that it seemed unquestionable. Like the correct conclusion to a mathematical sum, the idea of suicide was perfectly reasonable. It was just the solution to the theorem. Without my presence the world would be a better place.

Only a few small threads linked me to life. One was my love for my then cat, Fat Ada, a portly black and white moggie who moved in on me after living as a feral cat in my back garden. Ada was deeply neurotic and afraid of almost all human beings, especially men. She looked at a man's shoe as if it was likely at any time to kick her. Because of her unhappy early life she mistrusted every person in the world except me. Me she put up with and even loved. When anxious for affection she would walk up to me and flop down on the floor on her back – a heavy flop because of her weight. That morning I looked at Ada, lying on the floor hoping for a caress, and thought, 'You, at least, won't be better off without me.' She needed me.

The second thread was a surviving strand of common sense. It told me that I was ill in my mind. I had once before felt mad (in a different way, admittedly) so the idea that my sanity was crumbling was not new to me. Instead of telling my husband that I was going to kill myself for his sake, I said to him: 'I am very depressed. Please watch me and if you think I need it, admit me to a hospital.' Some part of me did not want to die. I was not quite ready to become the ultimate victim.

That day and others that followed it I had to be careful as I crossed the road. There was a desire simply to throw myself in front of a car and I knew that would be unfair to the driver. The habit of caring for others still seemed to be there; there was just no atom of caring for myself. I took taxis and buses instead of underground trains – the platform seemed too close to the inviting, deadly rails. I was in the early stages of working out how to commit suicide, not an easy task as I had to think of a way that would not upset others. Clearly getting someone else to run me over by car or train was too unkind. I also decided that I didn't want to overdose with drink and drugs. The drugs might be OK, but as a recovering alcoholic the drink was out, even as the ultimate mode of escape. The teetotal training held good: Do whatever you like but don't drink. How strange the human mind is *in extremis*.

I also made an appointment with a counsellor. I did it because it was the necessary thing to do since I acknowledged I was ill. It was the turning point to a second chance of life. In the first hour-long session with her, I told her all the blackest deeds I had ever committed. I told her about my worst sexual misdemeanours as a young woman, followed by all the drunken episodes later on that filled me with shame. I wanted her to know the full story of this creature sitting in front of her in her little office. I was dry-eyed. The early childhood inhibition, the self-censoring was still there – crying will only make people angry and everything will be worse. I also told her that I thought I might be going to kill myself. If she had showed the slightest apprehension about this, I think I would have left her room in even greater despair. I might even have done it. 'No, you are not going to kill yourself,' she said. It was her tone of voice, that of confident authority, which wove another thread that held me to life.

She told me to try and think of something nice about myself. After a great deal of thought, I could not think of anything at all. She said that I must. Then I came up with one virtue, that of persistence. I don't think it is my best virtue, but it is a quality which helped me to survive. Each time I thought of how disgusting I was, an inner voice intoned, 'But I have the virtue of persistence.' It drowned out the other voice urging me to remove myself from life. It kept me alive for a week until my next counselling appointment. But where was God when I needed him? At the time of my greatest need he was at his worst. Far from being a very present help in trouble, he was part of the agony, a big part of the dark cloud that was crushing me. The pattern was familiar from my childhood. Just like my poor father, who could not face other people's emotional pain and hit out at them when they were down, God was doing the same thing to me now.

His presence in my life was that of the Absolute Power who condemned people to hell. I had read 'Confessions of a Justified Sinner', about a man so certain of his salvation and his status as one of the elect, that he commits murder confident that he will still be saved. I was at the opposite pole. I was the damned, the un-elect, the person who was not chosen for salvation, the one already destined for hell by an inscrutable and merciless God. In this theology I could not save myself. 'You can't earn salvation', that earlier therapist had said to me. There was no way out. God had rejected me. Just as the elect can commit any sin, yet be saved, I could do any number of good deeds but would still go to hell.

During this terrible time it was therapy that rescued me. I began to see where the self-destructive behaviour came from. The Irish nanny, who had told me that I would go to hell, had somehow implanted a lasting message within me. When she arrived in our home in 1949, it was a difficult time for me. The long-awaited boy, the replacement for the defective girl, had arrived. I must have felt an outsider already. Now the handmaiden to the glorious new child was telling me I was beyond the redemption of God as well. No wonder I thought God did not love me.

My own father's lack of interest in me – the knowledge that I was the wrong sex, and indeed in other ways not the child he wanted – was now being played out in my adult mind when it thought of God. My father had been, of course, less vengeful than the God of my tortured understanding. But the child who was learning about God the father, already knew that her own father also appeared not to love her.

So in my five-year-old mind, I had constructed the father God as one who condemned me to eternal pain and who could not love me. The Jesuits claimed that if they had influence over a child up to the age of five, that influence would last for life. I suspect this is true. Like the duckling who follows the first moving creature or object, I had been 'imprinted' with this terrifying God. All the sophisticated aspects of my later religious education were merely layers of concealment over this. In my mind I was still the five-year-old who could not sing 'I belong to Jesus', because she knew it wasn't true, and who looked out at the farmyard, imagining herself dying and going to hell because she remained unbaptised.

We know now that childhood abuse can come back to haunt the adult. Battered or neglected children are marked for life by their experiences. Sexually abused children grow up to be victims of further abuse or, worse still, themselves become abusers. I had not grown up to be a spiritual abuser, thank goodness. I had not threatened others with hell, or used certainties as a weapon to hurt them. But the spiritual abuse of that Irish nanny, unwitting though it undoubtedly was, had changed my life for the worse. My deepest inner response to God was defined by it, wounded by it, and permanently disabled by it. It could be said that I was a spiritual abuse victim in need of healing.

Slowly I began to heal. At first I did not dare turn to the church for help. I had once, a couple of years earlier, when depression gradually began to overwhelm me, asked my then vicar if I could consult him on a spiritual problem. I wanted to ask him about my growing guilt and sense of inadequacy. But when I went to see him, his evident embarrassment and fear were so tangible that I felt unable to speak freely to him. When I arrived, he took me into his office and his wife came in to sit in the room with him. Did he think I was going to make a pass at him, I wondered? It was a thought that made me feel rather sick. I talked briefly and got out of the house as quickly as possible. Now in the true depths of self-hatred, I could not risk consulting anybody other than the completely reliable and kind. I was so fragile, I had to guard myself against others.

I discovered then and in other encounters that many people do not know how to respond to extreme emotional pain. Some of them simply laughed off my distress and tried to 'cheer me up'. This was hateful but not too harmful. Others decided they had solutions. These people were busy thinking up remedies, and these remedies were a way of stopping me telling them how terrible I felt. They could not face my pain, I suppose. Sometimes they would almost force solutions on me – a book to be read or a prayer to be said. Why hadn't I done this? they would ask, or, if I had, why had it not worked? There were also those to whom counselling or therapy is very threatening. They tried to warn me off it because of their own deep fears.

Worst of all were those who said I was the cause of my

own depression, because I wasn't doing the right things. Did I think God condemned me? Well, that was my fault for thinking that. Why didn't I trust him? Not trusting God was a sin. And, for those already in despair, being told that their despair is a grave sin is devastating.

My childhood had taught me how to tiptoe round others, so as to avoid their anger. I went back to that old skill, lying to people who I thought might try to bulldoze me into taking up their remedies, or simply tell me off. I kept my depression to myself as much as possible. I was even more secretive about counselling. This cut off potential sources of help from friends, but was safer than risking picking the wrong confidante.

I still went to church and said meaningless sentences to the vicar as he stood by the door when I left. Sometimes I cried in the pew, making sure I cried silently, like I had done as a baby, so that nobody would know. I stopped saying conventional prayers. They simply fed the image of the sinner confronted with the overwhelming God of wrath. I love Cranmer's prose, but during that first year of recovery I was grateful that my then church did not use the 1662 prayer book. Modern versions skim the surface of the relationship with God, but this surface gloss helped ease my tormented mind. I didn't want to be close to God. He was part of the problem rather than the solution.

I went on going to church in the same spirit that I continued my working life and most of my social life during this time. I clung to doing what I had always done, because if I had stopped doing it, I might not be able to start again. Once my husband had left for work, I might begin the day curled up in a foetal position on the floor in the corner of our dining room, crying like a baby. Sometimes I would rock myself there, head down, hugging my body, like the neglected children in Romanian orphanages. This stereotypical behaviour was curiously comforting, as it must have been for the orphans, though it distressed my feline saviour, Fat Ada. She didn't like seeing me cry. Sometimes I had to shut her out of the room, so that I could purge my pain in this way without upsetting her. Then, after twenty minutes of rocking, with or without tears, I could probably get back to my word processor and write my newspaper column about pets.

The day that had started with the weird rocking movement might end with me going out to a dinner party consisting of government ministers and other high powered people. At other dinner parties, I would sit there and listen as right-wing journalists around me on the third bottle of wine brayed about counselling as a lot of nonsense, or derided therapy as something fit only for weaklings. I would keep very quiet indeed. These ordinary social occasions were as painful as they had been when I was a sixteen-year-old. I coped, I think, because I had been brought up to take such ordeals in social life for granted, as something which had to be endured. As an adolescent I had been to dinner parties with my father, with instructions on how I must keep the conversation going. After dinner, he would deliver harsh judgments on my inadequate social skills so that I would try to do better on the next evening out.

When people were kind to me on such evenings, as some friends were (perhaps sensing my pain beneath the façade), I would feel an amazed gratitude. I could not understand how they could bear to talk to me. I had to remind myself that they didn't know about the rocking. I moved through these occasions like a zombie, apparently a normal person in other people's eyes, merely disgusting in my own. The words that came out of my mouth in what is called 'making conversation' were luckily disconnected from my true, tortured self.

Yet slowly I moved away from the shadows. I even managed to shed tears in front of my counsellor. From feeling that I should kill myself to relieve the world of my loathsome presence, I merely felt that it would have been better if I had never been born in the first place. I became not a blot which had to be scrubbed out, merely a useless mistake. This was a relief. I knew from my mother's account that my conception had indeed been an error. I knew also that my birth had nearly killed her. I knew, as I had always known, that I was not the son my father had wanted. This, my painful childhood, was discussed and examined in therapy not with the aim of attributing blame to the father and mother I loved and still love, but with the hope of taking away its power in my mind, so that it could no longer harm me in the present.

I had for many years forgiven them, if forgiveness were needed, but now, if I was to survive, I had to hold them responsible for how they had behaved during my childhood. Ordinary forgiveness had been useful in sustaining my relationship with them for the past eleven years, but it had not enabled me to forgive myself. Somewhere deep in my heart I was still blaming myself for not being the child they wanted, for being the family coward, the cuckoo in the nest, the runt of the litter. I had to see that these harsh judgments made by my parents had been due to their inadequacies, not my own. I arrived at a deeper forgiveness which embraced both them and me. All this was done within the privacy of my therapist's office. My parents were then still alive, and transferring the legacy of unhappiness from myself to them was not what I wanted. I did not ever tell my father about my depression; he was in his last year of life and very frail. I told my mother, but only a very diluted version of what was happening to me.

I also had to turn away from the God of condemnation. I dropped a lot of Christianity theology like unwanted baggage, not necessarily for ever, but certainly for a long time. Traditional Protestant theology seemed likely to kill me so, true or not, it had to go. If there was a God, to whom theological concepts were important regardless of the consequences to my mental health, then that was the same tyrant God of my depression. I didn't need him. Better no God at all than one resembling Hitler or Stalin with his camps in hell. If that God exists, then all truly humane people must surely turn away from him anyway. Each time he came into my mind, I would try to push him out of it, substituting other thoughts. I had to trust that God would understand if I had to reject him. Once again, to find God I had to abandon him. This time it was a matter of my life or my death.

I remember in particular one of the days when I felt I was doomed to eternal torture. I rang sympathetic friends. I talked for hours on the phone to them, but I could not somehow get this idea out of my head. Then I caught hold of these words, 'For thou lovest all the things that are, and abhorrest nothing which thou hast made.' I said them over and over again to myself until at the end of the day the gaping maw of hell was closed. I had drowned out the clamour of the underworld by sheer repetition of this text.

A loving God came slowly back. The first sign was not my continued presence in church on Sundays: that was just the outward form of the 'normal' façade. No, my journey back to God started with empty churches. I had always loved them and as an atheist usually visited churches when I was passing through towns or villages. Now, as I passed through London, I would drop into a church for perhaps two minutes. I did not pray. I did not dare to, any more than I dared tell my ordinary friends what was happening to me. I would merely sit there for a while. Sometimes I would cry. Then I started saying, 'I am here, God.' Just those four words. It was my first prayer in my new life.

What did I mean? These were, I think, words which suggested a little measure of self-acceptance and some tentative contact. Sometimes I would go to the statue of the Virgin in Westminster Cathedral and light a candle and sit for a minute in front of her. To me she represented the feminine principle within God. She still does and, Protestant though I am, I still go there occasionally to light a candle, when I feel I need to take a specifically female problem to God. But the female principle in God was only of limited help. Mother Julian of Norwich had talked of the motherhood of God, but if I simply made God the Father into God the Mother, it would not be the solution. For me a mother figure is forever connected with the idea of a victim, like my real mother. To change a tyrant God into a victim God, was to encourage the victimhood within me. I have asked myself why Jesus Christ was not available to me at that difficult time. For he was not. For a time I had to drop

Jesus Christ, as part of the Christian doctrinal load I could no longer carry. The sight of his tortured body hurt me: on the cross, in the stained glass windows, in the crucifixes attached to bare church walls, on the cards in the gift shop at the Cathedral, on the representations of the stations of the cross. If I let myself gaze at that dying figure, it was as if his pain entered into me and mixed with my pain. To bear this dual weight of grief was too much for me. I know that to have a God who suffers with you can be a comfort, but I didn't find it comforting then or, sometimes, now.

On the contrary: I was sensitised to other people's pain by my own. I suffered with unhappy dogs dragged around by thoughtless people. I suffered with children crying or being shouted at by irate mothers in supermarkets. I suffered with London pigeons which had rotting claws or even missing legs. One day I found a dying pigeon outside a London church and knocked at a vicarage door, hoping somebody might take it in and care for it. 'Leave it to God,' said a church worker, passing by on the other side as I suppose we all do at times. Eventually I stole a brick out of the vicarage garden and killed the poor bird to put an end to its agony.

I love cats and there were days when I felt as if I was experiencing the pain of every homeless feline stray in South West London. It was almost too much. I could not be a good Samaritan to every suffering little creature. I had felt my mother's pain in childhood; I was feeling it again now. As a child I could comfort her. Now I was too fragile to comfort anybody, though in her case I still tried my best with visits and phone calls. I had only a little comfort in myself to give to others. I had almost none for myself.

But the empty stillness of churches was calming and gave

me some moments of peace of mind. As I began to feel better I worked out a morning prayer. It consisted of visualising myself back in my childhood home, in the same farmyard where once I had imagined myself dying and going to hell. Only this time, I was there as an adult and also as a child. I took the child by the hand, and we walked together towards a great light which was God. There were no words, no self-examination, no repentance, simply a few seconds in that light. The light shone on me. It was a loving, accepting light.

I made no attempt to pray in the evening. This was too close to reviewing the day. I did not want to examine myself since I would always have found myself wanting, which would have set off another bout of self-loathing. Nor did I want to praise God. That seemed too much like praise given to a tyrant, or flattery offered to a deity who must be appeased. Anything which encouraged me to see God in that way had to be jettisoned to keep my sanity afloat. I had to presume that a loving God would not wish me to commit suicide, and would thus understand my many rejections of him.

Though I dared not (perhaps unfairly) trust my own vicar, a friend recommended another one. I turned up to see him by appointment and his secretary told me I must wait. I was in such a bad way that I could not keep up the façade of normality in front of what seemed her disapproving eyes. So I told her I would wait in the church, and went and cried there. The vicar came to find me, took me home, gave me a cup of tea and I told him that I felt terrible and that Christianity was a burden, not a comfort. 'It's all about pain and suffering and seems to tell you that you should be suffering too. If Christ was a victim then perhaps I ought to be a victim too.' I don't think I was very coherent with words and, oddly enough, I don't remember exactly what he said. I don't even remember his name. But I left feeling comforted, for he had listened to my complaint against God, accepted it without being shocked or angry, and had given me a text from Isaiah, about God's love.

Fear not; for I have redeemed thee; I have called thee by name; thou art mine.
When thou passest through the water, I will be with thee; and through the rivers, they shall not overflow thee: when thou walkest through the fire, thou shalt not be burned; neither shall the flame kindle upon thee...
Since thou wast precious in my sight, thou hast been honourable, and I have loved thee...
Fear not, for I am with thee.

There was also another verse:

Listen, O isles, unto me; and hearken, ye people, from far; The Lord hath called me from the womb; from the bowels of my mother hath he made mention of my name.

An odd verse to save me so much pain, but it helped me turn round the feeling that I was a mistake from the beginning of my life onwards. True, my mother hadn't wanted to get pregnant. True, I had been a disappointment to my father from birth. But perhaps God himself had called me by name in my mother's womb, recognising me from my earliest weeks. Perhaps he, if not they, wanted me to be born. Indeed, perhaps their lack of enthusiasm was proof, not that I was a mistake, but that I was a special-born, required to be in the world and so born despite their wishes. Primitive thinking maybe, but depression is not something that can be intellectually reasoned away. It has to be *felt* away, and this idea helped.

My other comfort was the beauty of the world. When I had first given up alcohol, I had witnessed the great glory of nature. I noticed the colour of leaves, the shadows in hedges, the glint of sunlight on the leaf, the rhythmical percussion of falling rain. Then, as I became used to ordinary life, this extra perception had left me. The shades of the prison house in my own mind, had slowly closed about me, cutting off all hope, happiness and real awareness of beauty.

Now the perception had returned. Though each day was full of painful thoughts, each day also brought this visual joy. I began to notice the loveliness of the world, without feeling that I was not entitled to be part of it. One day I saw a red fire engine racing through the streets on an emergency call, and I felt its beauty deep in my heart – its shiny red carapace with the light bouncing off it. If I lay on grass I thought of 'the delighted insects' described by the poet John Clare, another sufferer from depression. I felt closer to, and perhaps accepted by, the unspeaking creatures and inanimate objects of this world.

For a long time I kept a pebble in my pocket to remind me of God's love for all created beings. I had picked it up at a time when I was thinking of this love. It was complete and whole and it was loved by God. It had its own beauty, gleaming when wet, with a satisfyingly smooth texture in the palm of the hand. If a simple pebble could deserve this love, then so could I. I was nothing much, but then neither was a pebble, so I was worth a pebble. I kept it for two or three months, until I no longer needed it and lost it. I have felt a debt of special gratitude to pebbles ever since. Occasionally I still pick one up and keep it for a few days to remind myself of God's love.

Someone used the words 'the growing edge of trees' in my presence, a phrase that struck a chord with me. I would look up at the trees and see their growing tracery against the sky. I was the observer, yet I felt almost as if I was the tree. It was as if the beauty around me went straight into my veins, just as music once had done. The barriers between me and the world were paper-thin, as if I was connected to everything that existed. This brought all the pain of stray cats and wounded pigeons, but it also brought all the joy of the tree with its silhouette against the grey London sky. There is a temptation to lie and say my depression gave me great religious insights. It didn't. Even had it done so, they would not have been worth the agony I went through. Joy came with the pain, but the price of that joy, of that perception of beauty, was so costly that I would not knowingly choose to pay it again.

The pain did, however, help me towards a small spiritual breakthrough. For the first time I told God, as I had been unable to tell my real father, when I was angry. About eight months after I had first gone for help for depression, my cat Fat Ada started losing weight. She grew so thin that the pads of her feet dwindled and her claws would clatter across the floorboards like a strange bird. She was too weak to jump on to the furniture, too weak to go outside. The vet diagnosed FIV and told me that she had developed cancer because her immune system had broken down. She who had saved my life was losing hers. In the vet's surgery we said goodbye for the last time.

I raged against God. If I had cried in church for sorrow, my tears were now tears of anger and bitterness at the Almighty. I wanted to murder God for depriving my fat feline saviour of her life at the relatively young age of eight years. I railed at him in my prayers. They were not polite prayers. I cursed and swore at him. For the first time I failed to do the correct thing, failed to smother my anger, or to accept the will of God. I had no truck with those platitudes about how everything is for the best, or how there is a lesson in all adversity. Poor Fat Ada had been deprived of her life, and no spiritual lesson to me justified that loss. My prayers were prayers of accusation, rituals of abuse, howls of outrage. For the first time ever, I think, I showed absolute spiritual honesty towards God. There was no bullshit. I spoke to him exactly as I felt.

It wasn't until several months later that I realised the implications of my behaviour – I trusted him. My anger, fully expressed, showed that. I trusted him to understand. I trusted him not to zap back with eternal hell because of my anger. I began to feel that God might be a big enough person to take my anger and still love me. In this way, in the death of a cherished cat, and in my own fury about it, I had finally come to a conviction of the love of God.

CHAPTER TWELVE

A DEEP AND
DAZZLING DARKNESS

Like others who have survived the hell of depression I felt the need to look back and find ways in which the nearly unendurable agony was worthwhile. I won't let myself believe that God 'gave' me depression to teach me useful lessons; it's too disgusting a view of the Creator. Yet when I look back at that time and think how poor Fat Ada saved my life, I can see that her presence in my life was God-given. Why should God with a divine ingenuity not work through a portly black and white cat, or a Jewish therapist with long dangling earrings, or the growing edge of trees, or a single pebble held in the palm of my hand? God is down here as well as up there.

Of course there may be as many theological difficulties with a God down here, as one up there. After all, if God was in the glorious red colour of a speeding fire engine, was he not also in the agony of a stray cat or a crying child? And if he is in suffering, as well as beauty, perhaps there is less comfort in the thought of a God down here. My thinking mind, if it is not careful, can turn a comforting idea into a useless one by perceiving these intellectual difficulties. I have to beware of my thinking. If there is to be a loving relationship with God, it is my heart, not my intellect, which should play the major part. And to my heart, the idea of a God experienced through the things of this world, is a reassurance. Perhaps my relationship with God *is* a thing of shreds and patches, incoherently knitted together to make myself feel better; do the inconsistencies matter?

Another paradox is that I should never have rediscovered God but for all the whiskies I had drunk and the embarrassing and unkind actions I had committed. In my life it was sin (or a maladjusted personality) that pushed me towards God in the first place. If I had been a whole person, living a happy and reasonably well adjusted life, I should never have needed God in the first place. As somebody once said to me: 'Christ found me in my brokenness and lives in my powerlessness'. So what is this God who works through sins as much as he works through good actions? What of the people hurt by my unkind actions? Do they have to be hurt so that I can get back to God? Just to say all things work to the good in God's plan has to be a smug cop-out. Yet the thought that sin, as well as virtue, can be a road to God, has helped me stop trying to Be Good all the time. I can't be, and the effort involved seems to crush me. Living in a prison house of my own making, in which all words have to be censored and all feelings restrained, nearly killed me. Being Good was even worse for me than drinking too much. It threatened to rob me of life itself. It made self-acceptance completely impossible.

I also had to let go of compulsive helping. Under the guidance of my therapist, I once drew up a list of every action I had 'done for others' in a week. I think I wrote down about thirty actions in a fairly average seven days. Looked at carefully, about a quarter of these 'helping' actions were not wanted by the recipient. They were not so much the outflowing of spontaneous generosity on my part, as the inner compulsion to be of use. A further quarter of them were possibly useful to the recipient but, balanced against my own welfare, not worth the effort. Some of the people I was 'helping' were passive people who used others to address their insatiable inner needs. One lonely person I tried to help, would happily accept my visits but would not make any steps (even easy and obvious ones) to change her loneliness. At last I noticed this. I still visited her but I now had the knowledge that she had in a way chosen her solitary life, despite complaining about it. So I visited her when I chose, rather than out of a desire to ease her loneliness.

Once I recognised my helping compulsion, it threw light on one of my friendships. This was a friend who rang me up often. For the first time I noticed that each telephone call, after a certain amount of friendly chat, would involve his asking for something – help with his journalism, a phone number or a contact. Friends are there to help each other, so in itself this didn't necessarily matter. However, an occasion arose in which I wanted him to lend me a tape he had recorded. I asked for it and, without explanation, he refused. It occurred to me that perhaps this friendship was more convenient for him than for me. On his next two calls, I experimented with a pretext for refusing to give him the help he wanted. Our friendship had been one of my giving and his taking. As a compulsive helper, it had suited me well. Now that I was trying not to be one, the friendship no longer had any meaning for me, nor apparently for him. He never called again.

Spiritual honesty to others still eludes me. When I consider that giving-taking friendship, I wonder if I should have been more honest in my dealings with him. Perhaps I should have risked explaining what I thought was going on rather than simply dropping, and being dropped by, the 'friend'. My craving for approval and fear of disapproval too often makes me pretend to be nice, saying dishonest things to others, acting in dishonest ways, or evading the truth of an encounter as I did then. I still find it almost impossible immediately to say no to a request for help. The best I can manage is to ask for time to think about it, which gives me the chance to marshal my courage to say no.

Even changing my mind about simple things is difficult for me. I feel that once I have said I will do something, this is graven in stone. Of course there are important commitments which should not be broken, but I feel locked into a course of action even in business affairs. If I need to ask a publisher for a later delivery date for a book, it may take me several days to pluck up the courage. And quite often I will shore up what should be a simple request with an unnecessary buttress of excuses. I now show the long letters of apologetic reasoning to my husband, who rewrites them into the simple requests they should be. This inability to ask for what I want, like the difficulty in saying no, stems from the desire to please, a desire which gets in the way of real honesty.

This people-pleasing also interferes with the honesty of telling others how I feel – essential feedback for a good relationship. In the ordinary course of acquaintanceship, this really doesn't matter. If I am angry about the behaviour of somebody that I do not know very well and need not see again, I can simply decide to have no further contact. But anger with a true friend should be expressed. There isn't any need to shout and scream and express the hurtful variants of accusations like 'You always do this' or 'You make me sick'. But keeping silent about such feelings is a deception. If my husband asks me to do something, and I agree to do it while seething inside about the request, I deceive him. He cannot know I am angry and therefore cannot decide if his request is unreasonable. I stay resentful at him even though my deception has not given him the chance of rectifying the situation. This is what I should acknowledge as dishonesty.

I try to fool myself that being nice in this way is a form of kindness. It isn't. And it gets in the way of strong relationships. The ideal is simply to tell him 'I feel angry at your request', but a little shouting and screaming would at least be spontaneously honest! I know all this, but my practice falls lamentably short of theory.

Sometimes my old habits simply need retuning a bit. The self-monitoring, which led to self-restrained imprisonment, can be relearned as self-care. I try to monitor myself not by a series of disapproving judgments and warnings, but with a series of kind thoughts about getting proper rest, enjoyment and relaxation. If I get enough of these, I am kinder and better to others without the need for any great effort. Compulsive helping, when I fall back into it, means I have no time for myself, no time simply to stop and stare and potter. Yet a relaxed, happy person is often a morally better, kinder person. We all know life-enhancing people who seem to do few good works but are a joy to be around, in contrast to those who are always working for others and whose company is a blight.

Self-denial for its own sake is simply bad for me. There are times when the right thing to do requires self-denial, but this comes perilously close to self-punishment and is to my mind (and I mean this literally) an abomination. Brought up to believe that 'being selfish' was a sin, I begin to think enlightened selfishness has a lot going for it. I try to learn from my fox-hunting father's commitment to enjoying himself, though my enjoyments are different. Some people may not need recreation and renewal. I need them, in order to stay sane.

Working too hard is another compulsion for me. Sometimes I groan to think that I have run through almost every kind of compulsive activity – smoking, impersonal sex, drinking, compulsive helping and now compulsive work. Busy activity interferes with a spiritual life, it seems to me. When I am too work-obsessed to find time for rest or recreation, too busy to notice the beauty around me, too busy to chat with a friend, too busy to take a walk, then I am misusing my life. Like sex or drinking, it is another way to blot out reality, to stop myself spending time with my true self, perhaps a way of covering up self-hatred. If I am busy doing, I cannot be. The temptation to do rather than to be is a sign that I am feeling bad about myself. Beneath the surface of a high achiever you will find a self-hater, trying to feel better by notching up achievements. So I have to add workaholism to my ways of evading God, me, and reality. I am still struggling with it.

Like many of my other difficulties, my obsession with achievement has its roots in my childhood. Trying harder, as I automatically do, is a gift my father gave me and I am both grateful for it and wary of it. I can see much good in my childhood, which I owe to him. Just as my sins brought me closer to God, so have my childhood problems and their sometime bitter fruit. My father's behaviour to me as a child made me feel that God could not love me. But, through the pain of this, it also brought me closer to a God who did.

I understand my father now in a way that I could not when I was a child. I have put away the childish fear of him and see him through the eyes of an adult. In fact I am closer to him after his death than during his life. After he died I found a miniature portrait of him as a baby in a locket set with pearls, and for the first time I grasped the idea that somehow life had changed this wide-eyed innocent child into the adult who beat his horses around the head and prodded them with cruel spurs. I also found a prayer book with the inscription: 'From Daddie and Mummie, Xmas 1911. To their dear little Darby.' That prayer book, given to him at the age of eight, is how his spiritual life had begun, yet it had ended with him lying in a hospital bed, knowing his death was imminent, and refusing even to greet a visiting vicar. An ordinary non-believer would at least have said hello; I think my father feared and loathed religion too much to do that. I have wondered what inner hurt, what spiritual unkindness from school or church authorities, or spiritual ignorance by his parents, had led to his insistent turning away?

Our relationship in life had a happy ending, in that I began to love him with a truly grown-up acceptance. Secure in the protection of my husband, at the age of 34 I finally stopped fearing my father. With the help of Christianity, I tried to put love where I thought love might not be, and found that love had been there all along. I could not trust him with any of my troubles or unhappiness, nor could he in turn ever trust me with some of his own real troubles that, after his death, I discovered he suffered. In all the forty-six years I knew him he never complained to me about anything. He had as little pity for himself as he had for others.

Even harmless topics could never be broached, as if a kind of silence had fallen over whole areas of life between us. My father, whose principal business of life was hunting foxes, had a surprising love of poetry. His bookshelves were full of poetry books, which I now possess. Yet after his death I realised I had never talked to him about poetry, even though we shared this enthusiasm. The reason was, I think, that it automatically came into the category of topics not suitable for discussion. Poetry is, after all, about the emotional side of life and this was the side of life that was off limits.

But there was love there. It was an odd relationship. I would drive to have dinner with him and my stepmother about once a month. My father would open a specially good bottle of wine for my husband and specially nice food would be eaten. Yet the conversation was more like the talk between friendly acquaintances, than between family. He would tell anecdotes and I would tell anecdotes. Nothing intimate was said, but through this ritual chat we expressed our love. In his last illness, half paralysed by a stroke, unable to read and fading fast, he worried about remembering my birthday and insisted on my stepmother giving me a generous cheque. It was an expression of his love. He had loved me at the end of his life even if he didn't at the beginning of mine.

After his death I discovered one good reason why he could not love me in those first few years of my life. The

A Deep and Dazzling Darkness

clue lay in the way he had called me 'the cuckoo in the nest', which I had interpreted as meaning I was somehow not the right kind of person. It was a more pointed remark than that. In the early years of my life, he had suspected I was not his child. My sister told me this after his death and my mother confirmed it (while declaring that there was absolutely no basis for this idea). So when my father had looked at me with dislike and contempt, it was not just that I was the second unwanted girl, the weakling of the family, the coward in his eyes. I was also possibly illegitimate, the cuckoo in the nest, somebody else's child foisted upon him to rear. Later, as I earned a place in his esteem by looking after my little brother, I think he changed his mind. I resembled my brother closely and both of us had his family's looks, rather than my mother's. When I reached the age of eight it must have become clear to him that I was his genetic daughter after all.

He never breathed a word of this to me. As a frightened child, I just feared him. Now as an adult, I honour his generous decision to keep the child within his family. It cannot have been easy for him. Calling me 'the cuckoo in the nest' was an insult aimed, I believe, at hurting my mother, not me. He stopped calling me this later on, either because he no longer believed it to be true or (I rather hope but am not quite sure) because he knew I might understand what he meant. He was an extremely difficult father to all his children, but at last I had discovered why he singled me out for special contempt. I like to think he was rewarded for his generosity to a supposed bastard. At the end of his life I was the child closest to him, though not the child dearest to him.

His ashes now rest on the bleak moorland of Exmoor,

where a huge granite stone commemorates him and his second wife. I feel a great love and tenderness for him. To understand all is to forgive all. By letting go of my anger towards him, I am at rest with those ashes. If I have dwelt upon his imperfections in this book, it is because they are part of me. They have partly made me what I am, and when I love myself properly I love his legacy in me as much as I love the happier side of my personality. I still see similarities in the bond I had with him, and in the bond I have with God. The old relationship with God, which led to my breakdown, was one of the child with the dominating and unloving father. The new relationship I have with God is like the one I had with my father in later life – not intimate but, nonetheless, loving. It is far from perfect, an attenuated version of the closeness that should exist between God's child and God. But this attenuated relationship is better than the old one and represents considerable spiritual growth.

When I am in trouble God no longer threatens me, but he still seems not to be there when I am in a crisis. Four years after my father's death, my mother became ill with cancer and for a year I spent a lot of time caring for her. It was enormously tiring and I was often exhausted. I was driving hundreds of miles a week, getting very little sleep and almost no recreation. When returning from visiting her, I would have to stop off the motorway every twenty minutes or so, in order not to have an accident. I would get out of the car, walk up and down in the fresh air, slap myself several times on the face, eat sweets and drink cola before continuing my journey. At weekends, I often missed church to lie late in bed in the morning or sleep in the afternoon. I needed that rest in order to carry on and I felt no guilt. This lack of guilt arose from my trust, not so much that God would forgive me, but that he would understand my priorities so that his forgiveness would be unnecessary.

During this grim time, he receded. He still wasn't a very present help in trouble, but at least he did not add to it by being a threatening presence. I understood that for me God may well recede when I need him, because I cannot and will not ever be able to understand his fatherhood properly. My perceptions have been blighted forever since I now see God through the prism of my father's early relationship with me. 'For now we see through a glass, darkly; but then face to face.' If God is not apparently there when I need him, this does not mean that he is not present. I need not fuss about his absence.

Nor do I need to try to change or improve our relationship. Trying is bad for me. It is a variation on the old compulsions, the desire to please driven by fear of not pleasing. I aim to let go and let God. Just because I cannot make our relationship better does not mean that he cannot. If I stop trying to do it all, perhaps there will be space for his grace to work. 'I can't; you can,' I have prayed at times when I was facing difficulties over which I seemed powerless.

Indeed, the more I let things be, the happier I seem to be. It is as if my frantic activity and strenuous attempts to better my spiritual life, act in reverse. Does it matter if I don't believe much if God still loves me? I have let go my lack of belief. My only important belief is in universal salvation. That I must cling to because I cannot afford to believe in hell, for the sake of my emotional well-being. It would be insane to insist on a belief in hell if it can drive me nearly to suicide. Nor can I contemplate hell for those I love. Must my father, who turned with such force against a hurtful religion that he could not even greet the visiting vicar when he was dying in hospital, be damned eternally for lack of the correct theological belief? I love him still and the very idea makes me angry. What kind of God is it that gives punishment without healing after death? I cannot, will not, must not, believe in a God who permits hell to exist. The God I want and need is the God who would have a special concern for those who rejected him, who would understand the hurt which lay beneath this turning-away.

Most of the time I cannot wholeheartedly assent to the major Christian truths – the Virgin birth, the godhead of Jesus Christ, the resurrection and the Last Judgement. Only now I do not fuss about my heresies. What is an opinion, after all? Only a fleeting impression upon my intellect. My lack of belief doesn't change the truth or untruth of these ideas. If faith is about believing in the 'right' theological concepts, then I don't have it. But if faith is trusting God then I am beginning to acquire it. A loving God is not going to love me less because I do not believe. Indeed he might love me more, finding my lack of belief amusing, as I find my cats' bad behaviour part of their charm. For it seems to me my relationship with my cats, who are lower down the scale of intelligence, has something of the relationship I have with God. Only I am the cat and he is far further above me. (Incidentally, I do not make the mistake of thinking I am worth more to God than a cat or, for that matter, a pebble. Each created thing is worth a whole universe. There is a world of love in a pebble, as I know.)

A Deep and Dazzling Darkness

I am hopeless at prayer. I find it boring. When I kneel down, or sit down, or even lie on my back to pray, the first thing my mind does is to go somewhere else. It doesn't want to pray. It has no interest in, or enthusiasm for, praying. I can trick it by repeating a prayer learned by rote, though my mind may wander while I do this. Sometimes I can trick it by visualisation. I don't picture episodes in the life of Christ, as some Christian writers have suggested. If I do, I just see this awful wet Jesus figure, usually blonde, surrounded by white males. I also tend to site myself among the baddies rather than the goodies in the scene and this makes me rebellious rather than devout.

I still use my own childhood as a place to find God. I imagine myself as the child I was, in the farmyard of my childhood, walking towards a light – my Father in heaven who accepts me as I am. I can also sometimes manage to hand over the day to him. I picture lifting it up, or giving him my daily list of things to do. But sometimes in the middle of this, my mind runs away and starts worrying about the day ahead. The moment of prayer has been five seconds, the worry is five minutes before I catch it on the wing and stop it.

I cannot praise God in prayer with much enthusiasm either. Somehow it still smacks of flattery or the behaviour of a servile courtier. So instead I cultivate wonder, which enriches my life. A day without a single minute's wonder is a day in which my spirit is impoverished. If I walk out into fresh rain, driving snow, fog or sunlight, I can marvel and rejoice at its beauty. Having to praise God for it seems like paying tribute, a tax on my enjoyment. Pure wonder is pure enjoyment, which is my prayer. I love seeing my cats enjoying their food: I don't want them to thank me for it. So I hope God accepts my sense of wonder. I have been created not for unhappiness and stern moral purpose: I have been created to 'live out my life as a happy child in the sunshine of God's love,' as Father Mo once wrote to me all those years ago.

Am I a Christian? If being a Christian means believing in the catechism or the creed, then I definitely am not. If being a Christian means imitating Christ and bearing his cross, then I fear I am not. I do not dare. If being a Christian is practising gentleness and mercy and love, then I wish I were one but I am not. I try but often fail to do these things.

I am a Christian only because I call myself one. If I do not fit into the boundaries of Christianity, then God will take me in anyway. I may be a kind of outcast or a loner, or even a wilful self-excluder, yet God will still include me. What we know of the life of Jesus Christ is that he had a special care for the outcast, the misfit, the sinful and the poor. So in that sense I qualify triumphantly as a Christian and nobody can take my 'membership' away from me. Besides, at the core of my spiritual life, is my need for Christianity. I have complete faith in my need. God I often have doubts about, but I have no doubt about my need for him.

I admit that much in this book is a muddle. Many readers will want to say that I haven't properly understood various matters, that the answers lie in more conscientious Bible study, in more Christian discipline, in greater commitment from myself. I know that there are intellectual answers to many of my questions. I know that if I could open up to other Christians I would benefit from this. But I fear other people's certainties: they hurt so, and my heart is not satisfied with answers or Bible study. 'The heart has its reasons which reason knows nothing of,' wrote Pascal. In this book I have tried to write the story of my true heart, not my educated mind. It is in my heart that I need love, not answers.

In February 1995 I had a dream. It was not an ordinary dream. I would describe it as being more like experiencing reality, except that it was far more vivid than ordinary reality. I was in a happy clappy church, looking on as an observer at an excitable congregation. A great white light exploded outwards from inside my breast – bright not hot, but the explosion was painful. My instinctive reaction was to try to keep the light in and stop it breaking out. I thought it would shatter my breast with its power. I heard the flapping of huge wings, like the wings of a swan. Then I said to myself, in the dream, 'It is the Holy Ghost. I must not shut it out. I must try to keep myself open to it.' My legs collapsed and I slid to the ground with my back against the wall. Then I was conscious of the happy clappies crowing round my fallen body saying that I shouldn't be like this, I should be joyful, extrovert, rolling around. Yet all I felt was fear and distress. In this dismay I woke up.

The dream troubled me. It woke in me the thought that I was, once again, showing my inadequacy. I wondered if I should have a second attempt at trying to push myself into the 'right' Christian mould – praying properly in the approved Church fashion, practising constant gratitude and cheerful acceptance of God's will, evangelical fervour and correct theological certainties. Perhaps it was not good enough to sidle up to God like a nervous horse approaching a doubtful object. Perhaps it was wrong to prefer God down here more than up there.

And yet if the dream was a message, it was a message modified by my own mind. My thinking is founded on doubt and pain. I have a friend whose religious experience came with the sound of a swan's huge wings. For her, the feeling was one of total confidence in God's love. I don't think my mind could transmit that confidence. It doesn't have the wherewithal. In my case, the software, developed in the first five years of life, has been geared to a different mode altogether. Perhaps I only recognise God in pain, or perhaps I only recognise him *with* pain.

This dream suggested two things to me. The first was that there is in God a deep and dazzling darkness, an otherness of mystery and awe, a power and authority so immense that it is natural to fear it, to experience it as a shattering of the safe and the familiar. This aspect of God I have turned away from, because I dare not, for my own sanity, face it. My attenuated relationship with God is domesticated, even cosy. I talk to a friend that I do not fear. To achieve this intimacy, to find a little place of safety with God, I have had to lose the sense of his power, authority and mystery. I must remember that this loss is my choice and my God does not represent the totality of his nature. The awesome mystery and power of God the Almighty still exists, even if I have to close my eyes to it.

The second lesson that the dream taught me was that perhaps my spiritual way, the way that can be trodden by me, is not the eternal way. I have achieved, after healing childhood hurt, some spiritual safety, but what if safety is not enough? I cling to it because I am frightened of anything worse. Must I let go even of this? I dare not do it now. Perhaps I never will dare in the future. So I trust in God to understand me, to forgive me, and to continue loving me, however far I go astray.